CORPORATE CELEBRATION

CORPORATE CELEBRATION

PLAY, PURPOSE, AND PROFIT AT WORK

TERRENCE E. DEAL & M. K. KEY

Berrett-Koehler Publishers, Inc.
San Francisco

Berrett-Koehler Publishers, Inc.

450 Sansome St., Suite 1200
San Francisco, CA 94111-3320
Tel: (415) 288-0260, Fax: (415) 362-2512

Ordering Information

Individual sales. Berrett-Koehler publications are available through most bookstores. They can also be ordered direct from Berrett-Koehler at the address above.

Quantity sales. Special discounts are available on quantity purchases by corporations, associations, and others. For details, contact the "Special Sales Department" at the Berrett-Koehler address above.

Orders for college textbook/course adoption use. Please contact Berrett-Koehler Publishers at the address above.

Orders by U.S. trade bookstores and wholesalers. Please contact Publishers Group West, 1700 Fourth Street, Berkeley, CA 94710. Tel (510) 528-1444; 1-800-788-3123; fax (510) 528-3444.

Cover and Interior Design Barbara Gelfand

Printed in the United States of America

Printed on acid-free and recycled paper that is composed of 85% recovered fiber, including 15% postconsumer waste.

Library of Congress Cataloging-in-Publication Data

Deal, Terrence E
    Corporate celebration : play, purpose, and profit at work / Terrence E. Deal & M. K. Key.
       p. cm.
    Includes bibliographical references and index.
    ISBN 1–57675–013–2 (alk. paper)
    1. Corporate culture. I. Key, M. K., 1949–   . II. Title.
HD58.7.D418   1998
658.3'14--dc21

                                98–4453
                                   CIP

05 04 03 02 01 00 99 98   10 9 8 7 6 5 4 3 2 1

DEDICATION

This book is dedicated to all the courageous leaders—past, present, and future—who are infusing America's organizations with passion, purpose, and joy. Their efforts reap benefits beyond a robust bottom line: They are giving people an opportunity to find meaning at work.

TABLE OF CONTENTS

PREFACE

This book started to gel for both of us nearly twenty-five years ago. For Terry, the initial stimulus was a 1970s study conducted at Stanford University, for which he was one of the researchers who came to the then-startling conclusion that people's behavior in organizations is shaped only minimally by formal structure. That finding launched an expedition to explore the nonrational, inner workings of human organizations, which eventually led to his 1982 publication of *Corporate Cultures*, coauthored with Allan Kennedy. That book became an international bestseller, one of the first to introduce a powerful new way of thinking about American business.

Since that time, firsthand observations of corporate ceremonies across the world have deepened an appreciation for the power special occasions have to shape and reinforce cultural patterns and practices. His 1993 book with William A. Jenkins, *Managing the Hidden Organization*, highlights the role celebration plays in motivating people whose backstage work is critical to frontline performance. In 1995, the publication of *Leading with Soul* (with Lee Bolman) presented ritual and ceremony as key factors in summoning human spirit and creating a shared sense of significance among people.

During this same quarter century, M. K. was making her mark as a community psychologist and a creative, enlightened manager, excelling within industries as varied and change-wrought as oil and gas, entertainment, and the current monster—managed health care. She became convinced that ritual and ceremony are key components of quality and leadership. Her management roles and later consulting work in health care revealed to her just how important celebration can be in an industry besieged by change, cost cutting, and massive disruption. She was able to observe firsthand what people can do if given permission and a palette to create ritual and ceremony for a variety of occasions. As a seasoned consultant, she paved the way for new emphasis on celebration in the field of health care.

For us, this book is a capstone work, drawing on knowledge developed through many years of direct experience. Our observations have led us to an important conclusion: The time has come to refocus attention on the human side of organizations. Without ritual and ceremony, organizations quickly become sterile and devoid of meaning and buoyancy. If the 1980s and 1990s were decades of tightening up and reengineering, the new millennium will become a time of celebrating—a time to pump life and zest back into the workplace by making people a top priority and giving them a chance to tap their potential. Livening up rather than tightening down will become the key to greater profits. Celebration will help lead the way to economic prosperity.

Ironically, economic forces themselves laid the groundwork for a new emphasis on corporate celebration. During the 1980s and 1990s, foreign competition and other fiscal realities forced most American businesses to do some serious belt-tightening. Since the largest chunk of a company's financial liability is the cost of its people, workers were laid off in droves. Call it restructuring, downsizing, rightsizing, or whatever the prevailing euphemism, a lot of people found themselves out of work. Those who kept their jobs were left wondering when their turn would come. Coupled with new technology, mergers, alliances, and other disruptive changes, the end result was too often a demoralized, apathetic, and dispirited workforce.

Too often, however, the human costs of economic readjustments were overlooked. Rationally based economic thinking still continues to dominate the business world. The chief problem with this is that people are too often left out of the financial equation. Simply calling people human capital leaves something important outside the box. People have feelings, hearts, souls, spirits, and other nonrational qualities. When the workplace speaks to these, people voluntarily give their all. When the workplace ignores these nonrational qualities, people typically check out. They leave, strike, sabotage, or—more passively—just go through the motions.

Evidence is accumulating that shows how much human factors affect the financial bottom line directly and dramatically. And since every business is a people business, executives and managers are beginning to wake up to the realization that hefty financial payoffs require their devoting a lot of attention to the softer side of the workplace.

This book makes a case for the central role of celebration in reinvigorating and reinspiriting corporations. To be sure, having the right strategy and appropriate structure are also very important. But all corporate activity requires human energy to succeed, and human energy is fueled in large measure by ritual and ceremony. Always has been. Always will be. So to excel, captains of industry must now become champions of celebration.

This shift in thinking will not come easily. American managers are among the most rational in the world. Deep down, many would probably rather manage things than people. Things are predictable, efficient, relatively easy to control, and require only mechanical maintenance. People, on the other hand, are whimsical, political, and distracted constantly by emotions and pressures both inside and outside of work. People require loads of emotional support and want meaningful work as well as a bountiful paycheck. Herb Kelleher, CEO of Southwest Airlines, once remarked, "A friend's wife called me just after he assumed a top corporate position. She complained that he was spending 80 percent of his time on people issues. I told her that he must have landed a real cushy job. I spend 95 percent of my time dealing with people."

This book is written for managers and executives who are searching for better ways to develop and encourage people at work. It provides solid evidence and a grounded framework for identifying opportunities to celebrate. It shows how ritual and ceremony arise naturally around seasonal cycles, recognition, and moments of triumph. It also demonstrates how ritual and ceremony are just as appropriate for personal transitions and the unavoidable moments of corporate calamity and loss. It highlights altruistic efforts on behalf of others in the community as powerful celebratory occasions. It shows how play can restore elements of fun, zest, and joyfulness at work.

At the end of his career, quality guru W. Edwards Deming reduced his fourteen points for leaders to one key idea—the human spirit. And to us, the human spirit is summoned most majestically in ritual and ceremony, the celebratory side of life at work. This book provides general principles for setting the stage, orchestrating the process, and encouraging spontaneity in corporate celebrations. It also offers, tongue in cheek, some advice on how to kill an event.

For those looking for concrete answers, surefire recipes, and lockstep procedures, this book will be a major disappointment. But for those searching for ideas to help them shape a more meaningful work environment—emphasizing play and purpose as a promising pathway to profit—this book should be a welcome companion. Our experience clearly shows that the best answers to current challenges come from within rather than from without. The aim of this book is to stir up an internal dialogue, one that will eventually lead to more elegant conversations with others and ultimately to more meaningful and profitable human enterprise.

This book is aimed at a diverse audience across sectors, functions, and organizational levels. The message is just as relevant for a CEO of a multinational financial business as for a hospital executive or the principal of a large urban high school. It offers something just as important to the manager of an engineering division as to a marketing manager, to a research and development executive as to a foreman on the plant floor of a manufacturing operation. CEOs, department heads, team leaders, and MBA students should find these ideas a challenging call to action if they want their enterprises—and their careers—to succeed.

We have tried to include examples that cut across sectors, functions, and organizational levels. But through the years we have found that basic ideas about celebration are applicable to any human group. Our hope is that people everywhere will use this book as a springboard to create their own magic moments, making work more enjoyable, meaningful, and profitable.

Terry and M.K.
Nashville, Tennessee
February 1998

ACKNOWLEDGMENTS

Throughout this book, we praise the importance of celebration in the workplace. Ritual and ceremony provide special occasions to acknowledge and recognize people's efforts. In creating this work, we have been blessed with a rich array of people who have brought their gifts to us in a myriad of forms. Some are *visionaries*, who have shaped and inspired our thinking. Others are *storytellers*, who have guided us to sources and examples. A talented *supporting cast* has handled production details and other logistics. *Cheerleaders* have buoyed our spirits at critical times. *Critics* have polished and refined our ideas with us. For all of this help, we are truly grateful.

In keeping with our purpose, we imagine gathering all these individuals together for a special awards celebration. The invitation is a miniature hot air balloon that contains all of the travel arrangements. The setting is anywhere in this world that we can be together: It could be in nature, abundant with flowers and the sounds of water, full of fragrance and beauty. A program of celebration music is being played by a string quartet. Champagne, chardonnay, and sparkling cider flow. A colorful display of smoked sturgeon, caviar, and sushi invite a taste, along with a large chocolate-mousse cake and fresh strawberries for those desiring sweets.

Greeted lovingly by us, people join each other to mingle, quaff, and munch. Facilitators introduce people to one another, provoke discussions, and encourage dancing. The predominant feeling is one of gratitude and joy. "Together we have created this gift to the world." After much spontaneity and gaiety, people are invited to gather for a brief ceremony.

Against a large backdrop of the book cover behind the dais, we begin to address the group: "What you see here is a product of your efforts. As the authors, we simply assembled the good ideas. It would be nothing without you. We celebrate you and all that you have meant to us. We cannot thank you enough."

At this point, a small group of instigators reveals a surprise that we did not expect. They have put together a video of quips and stories, beginning with interviews with our parents—Robert and Dorothy Deal, Fred and Kathryn Key—without whose support we would not have had the will or the skill to take on such a challenge. Everyone tells little tales on us, and we all roar with laughter.

We resume our presentation, thanking the humorists and videographers (who are still at it, filming this whole event). "We first wish to thank our families, our sources of nurturance and support." We ask our parents and our spouses, Sandra Deal and Paul Whitehead, and our children, M. K.'s Carson and Terry's Janie, to come forward and stand by us.

"And for those of you who are visionaries—you have served as sources of continual inspiration and wisdom. Please accept this gift of a dream-catcher. Come join us—James Autry, Lee Bolman, Patsy Bruce, Janice Beyer, Harvey Cox, Max DePree, Matthew Fox, the Freibergs, Robert Fulghum, Bill Jenkins, Allan Kennedy, Rabbi Morris, Barbara Meyerhoff, Sally Moore, Harrison Owen, Kent Peterson, Mac Pirkle, Anita Roddick, Kathleen Ryan, Harrison Trice, and David Whyte. Let us also remember W. Edwards Deming for his great contribution.

"Storytellers, each in his or her own way, have guided us to the examples and anecdotes that lie at the heart of the book. Come forward and allow us to give you a token, a ceramic Sante Fe storyteller: Lori Brewer, Diane Cox, Donna Culver, Ruth Elder, Dennis Ford, Barbara Glanz, Janna Lewis, Elaine Millam, Sandy Murray, Bob Nelson, Burgess Olivier, Sue Fort White, Chris Vinh, Matt Weinstein, Joan Vydra, James Whitehead, Roy Williams, and many, many more.

"Reviewers—Frank Basler, Lorna Catford, Peter Grazier, Jennifer Myers, and Perry Pascarella—we thank you. This book would not be what it has become without you to hone our ideas. Please accept a year's supply of Post-its™ and colored pens.

"Too often, the efforts of the supporting cast are obscured. Tonight is a time to ask you to share the spotlight, accept our applause, and be recognized for the yeoman duties you performed. Come forward and accept a grant for your dream—Homa Aminmadani, Nathanial Bray, Vicki Spina. All the students who brought research—Jim Coaxum III, Karen Elsey, Jason Embry, Scott Fisher, Kim Hoenshell, Karen Key, Nancy Kiel, Koree Knight, Angela Malone, Amanda McElroy, Jennifer Nordloh, Marsha Palen, Caroline Portis, Nancy Price, Mark Robertson, Christine Robinson, Sara Stubblefield, Evans Whitaker, Jason Wolf, Christine Wu, Jubal

Yennie. The staff and course participants of the Center for Continuous Improvement at Quorum Health Resources, Inc. And all the people at Berrett-Koehler, with a special thanks to Mary Lou Sumberg and Elizabeth Swenson.

"Finally, we applaud our cheerleaders who coached us along when our energy or courage failed. This includes almost everyone we talked to about the book, who let us know how timely and needed it was. One editor in particular cried, 'Make it your bully pulpit,' and so we did. Another, Marian Prokop, spotted a hole in the leadership literature and we attempted to dive into it. Our families once more deserve our love and appreciation. And not to forget Steven Piersanti, our champion and editor at Berrett-Koehler. For all of you, we have a tape of specially arranged celebration songs.

"To everyone, a hearty thanks. We could not have done it without you. Along with the mementos you received, you will find a ticket permitting celebration anytime, anywhere. We want you to continue the spirit of this work everywhere you go."

The grand finale is set off by thunderous applause, the release of environmentally safe balloons, streamers, and confetti. People visit and play for as long as they care to, and when they choose to leave, receive again our personal thanks and their own copy of the book with a story of the special role they played.

PART ONE

The Case for Corporate Celebration

Chapter 1

Corporate Celebration: Frivolous or Fundamental?

The time: December 1991. The occasion: the annual Christmas party at Quad/Graphics—a celebration of the company's twenty-fifth anniversary. The theme: H.M.S. Printafour. The setting: fifteen hundred employees dressed in formal attire and assembled in a large auditorium with an orchestra to provide musical accompaniment. Harry Quadracci, Jr., the company's founder, is dressed in an admiral's costume and opens the event. After a brief introduction, a large eighteen-wheeler pulling a decorated flatbed trailer enters stage right. On it are the company's managers all dressed in sailor costumes. They open with a series of songs, backed by a twenty-one-piece orchestra. Harry Quadracci then sings the history of the company. The singing vice presidents do a takeoff on the song "There's Nothing Like a Dame." Their version of the lyrics: "There's Nothing

Like Our Jobs." Harry then presents awards to the people who have become "masters of the printing craft." Harry closes the event with the invitation, "Let's party!" And the entire company—executives and employees—wines, dines, and dances into the night.

This event is not unusual at Quad/Graphics. It happens every year—each time a full-scale corporate musical set to a different theme. Like many other top-performing companies, Quad/Graphics realizes that taking time to celebrate is an integral part of doing business. The cost of the gathering is offset by the subsequent dividends it reaps in employee morale, commitment, and hard work. Seasonal celebration summons the corporate spirit, creating energy that carries over into the new year. Celebration at Quad/Graphics is not a superfluous, superficial add-on. It is a cultural high point and plays a central role in the company's success.

But what happens when times are tough and things aren't so rosy? How can a company celebrate when its performance is on the rocks? What's to celebrate when the workforce is being downsized? How can you have a blast when your company has just been acquired in a hostile takeover? Too often, we overlook a more solemn aspect of ceremony: people often gather more tightly in the depths of despair than in the highs of success.

Think about Princess Diana's funeral. The controversy over whether the Union Jack would fly at half-staff over Buckingham Palace. The flowers. The funeral march with her casket passing in review on a horse-drawn carriage. The honor guard marching to the "dead man's" cadence. The bells tolling at one-minute intervals. Princes Philip and Charles along with her two sons, Princes William and Harry, joining the procession just before its arrival at Westminster Abbey. The hymns. Earl Spencer's moving eulogy. Tears. The procession leading to Princess Diana's final resting place. Tragedies cry out for healing events. As a September 16, 1997, *Newsweek* article noted, "To die alone is bad enough, but to grieve without rituals that lift a broken heart is worse" (p. 62).

Our society recognizes the importance of gathering together when times are tough. Otherwise, people disintegrate and pull apart. Ritual and ceremony create a hallowed sense of solidarity and optimism. Why can't companies follow society's lead and convene ceremonial occasions even when business is bad? Good ones do, as the following story illustrates:

The time: 1985. The occasion: The annual gathering of managers from the Hospital Corporation of America (HCA). The theme: The Big Tent Shuffle—dealing with straight quarters of disappointing financial performance caused by a major shift in health care reimbursement policies. The setting: All managers worldwide in attendance and large-screen televisions in each corner of the large ballroom. The CEO, Thomas Frist, Jr., foregoes his usual speech and instead introduces a video featuring the company's top executives dressed in football uniforms. The HCA "Bad News Bears" then execute a rousing musical rap set to the theme "We're so bad we know we're good." For the next five minutes, the company's successful past, less than satisfying present, and potentially robust future are dramatically—and hilariously—portrayed. When the executives finish their rap, the entire group participates in redoing the rap, taking its cue from lyrics flashed on the video screens.

Both Quad/Graphics and HCA exemplify an important precept once heeded by our ancestors, now too often cast aside: The ups and downs, comings and goings, triumphs and mishaps of corporate life must be punctuated periodically with ceremonial events. Otherwise, the collective spirit that unites people in a common quest begins to wither and wane. People are homo festivous, their lives dominated by a common yearning for special times and gala occasions. Without them, we diminish an integral part of our humanity.

In *Feast of Fools*, Harvey Cox observes that modern people often lose their gift for fantasy and festival. As a result, we all too often experience life as flat drudgery to be tolerated rather than as uplifting adventure to be embraced and savored. Celebrations infuse life with passion and purpose. They summon the human spirit. They reattach us to our human roots and help us soar toward new visions. They touch our hearts and fire our imaginations. They bond people together and connect us to shared values and myths. Ceremonies and rituals create community, fusing individual souls with the corporate spirit. When everything is going well, ritual occasions allow us to revel in our glory. When times are tough, ceremonies draw us together, kindling hope and faith that better times lie ahead.

Shortcomings of Today's Bottom-Line Mentality

If we look at today's corporate America, we see a frenzy of rightsizing, merger mania, tightening to get leaner and meaner, collapsing cultures in joint ventures and buyouts—all with the sole intent to make more profit, to acquire greater economic clout and an expanded market position. Today's emphasis is too often fixed solely on the quarterly return monitored by stock-watching shareholders and analysts. Who among us is inspired solely by the purpose of making the stockholders and corporate executives wealthier? Fewer now than ever.

In *The Credibility Factor* by James Kouzes and Barry Posner, the authors point to a crisis of confidence among American managers, fueled by scandals, betrayals, nearly obscene executive compensation despite lackluster corporate performance, quality problems, widely held suspicion of corporate motives, and rampant cynicism. More troubling, major disconnects have opened a wide rift between the laboring populous of the workplace and its leaders. According to Barbara Glanz in her book *Care Packages*, a March 1995 Roper poll found that employee morale and job satisfaction were at the lowest ebb ever—since Roper has been taking polls. Workers feel used; bosses are burned out. Although Scott Adams, creator of the cartoon strip *Dilbert*, is having a field day, those who work for a living don't always find their immediate situation quite so funny. According to Kouzes and Posner, the disciplines of credibility are sorely lacking, for example, appreciating constituents, affirming shared values, developing capacity, discovering your own self, serving a purpose, and sustaining hope.

Where are the watchdogs who champion meaningful work? Who is calling attention to the collective oomph needed to produce top-flight products or services? What has become of the human side of doing business? All businesses are people-driven, and to tap their full potential, people need more than a paycheck: They need meaningful work. A January 9, 1997, headline in the *Wall Street Journal*, "The Search for Meaning in Meaningless Work," shows that what's missing is truly being missed. For too many people, work just isn't fun anymore. Their concern is echoed by today's business writers.

In *The Reinvention of Work*, Matthew Fox draws a crisp distinction between jobs and real work. Jobs, meaningless work, derive from a mechanical paradigm— piecework where people perform a well-defined task purely for economic gain.

They check their heads at the door, do what they are told, and eagerly await Friday's paycheck. David Whyte, in *The Heart Aroused: Poetry and Preservation of the Soul in Corporate America*, finds the experience of joy in work so incredibly rare that when we experience it, we're not used to it. Joy is a vulnerable state, fleeting, a corollary of loss. Loss is manifest in grief, in the daily struggle, at the price of family and personal time. Our personal lives are sacrificed on the altar of a drab, joyless workplace. And we can never give enough. Organizations often demand more effort without creating more meaningful, motivating work. The prevailing equation is: Business = busyness.

To experience both joy and grief is to feel life's full experience, to crawl out of the seminumbness that most of us feel at work. The answer, for Whyte, is found in a poetic soulfulness—the palpable presence of sacred otherness in our labors. Work is a sacred compromise; at its best, it is a calling. Work has majesty, dignity, and grace. People do it because of its intrinsic worth as well as the economic benefits. As Studs Terkel commented in *Working*, his now classic survey of the American workplace

> [Work] is about a search too, for daily meaning as well as daily
> bread, for recognition as well as cash, for astonishment rather
> than stupor; in short, for a sort of life rather than a Monday
> through Friday sort of dying. Perhaps immortality, too, is part
> of the quest (p. xiii).

Many have called attention to our all-too-often sterile workplaces. Consider W. Edwards Deming's internationally acclaimed philosophy that spawned the widely heralded quality movement. But heeding did not always accompany the heralding. American managers only got part of the message. The focus on measuring quality stuck—at least for a while; but Deming's equally important emphasis on joy in work was forgotten or overlooked. (See Deming's own books, *Out of the Crisis* and *The New Economics for Industry, Government, Education*, as well as *The Deming Dimension* by Henry R. Neave and *Deming's Road to Continual Improvement* by William W. Sherkenbach.)

As we sought a publisher for this book, we found that the very idea of corporate celebration seemed an aversive subject for many. Too touchy-feely. Too frivolous for financially oriented managers. Besides, who would buy a book on fun and festivity when times are lean and managers ought to be mean? Who would pay money to learn the secrets of celebration when reengineering appears to be a more promising answer? What do festival and fun have to do with the financial bottom line?

If we review where business is today, we can see that massive corporate dollars are being spent on reengineering, strategic planning, consultants, and performance evaluations with little tangible evidence of any real payoff—either economically or psychologically. In *The Rise and Fall of Strategic Planning*, for example, Henry Mintzberg penetrates the rational mystique of that widely proclaimed corporate activity. He presents compelling evidence and vivid anecdotes, raising serious questions about whether strategic planning really progresses in a straight line from rational analysis to productive action. Still, companies continue to champion strategic planning even while many executives clearly recognize its shortcomings. Russell Ackoff, quoted in Mintzberg's book, comments

> Recently I asked three corporate executives what decisions in the last year they made that they would not have made were it not for their corporate plan. All had difficulty identifying one such decision. Since each of their plans was marked "secret," or "confidential," I asked them how their competitors might benefit from the possession of their plans. Each answered with embarrassment that their competitors would not benefit. Yet these executives were strong advocates of corporate planning (p. 98).

What's going on here? Why would executives continue to champion an activity with questionable tangible benefits? Perhaps deep down inside, they may realize that business needs a periodic boost from some kind of ceremony. But they are wary of advocating superfluous activity that might make them appear soft. So they wrap ceremony in rational packaging and let it do its work indirectly, appearing as something more conventional. J. B. Quinn makes this point in Mintzberg's book:

> A good deal of corporate planning I have observed is like a ritual rain dance; it has no effect on the weather that follows, but those who engage in it think it does. Moreover, it seems to

me that much of the advice and instruction related to corporate planning is directed at improving the dancing, not the weather (p. 139).

Are we observing ceremonial activity disguised as management control? Yes, but at least it provides a welcome change of pace in an often lifeless business enterprise. There is a valuable lesson here that even rational managers seem to endorse but may not admit readily: Overlooking the human, ceremonial side of an enterprise undermines gains made by any technical or external intervention.

Benefits of Celebration: A Long-Range View

Some corporate heads are waking up, stepping out, and taking a different tack. For example, H. R. H. Prince Philip, CEO of Liechtenstein Global Trust (LGT), was recently asked to put a dollar figure on a three-day, top-executive gathering in Whistler, British Columbia, which 120 company executives (plus spouses) from around the world attended—a sizeable investment by any standard. Without hesitating, he smiled and replied, "About half of what it would have cost to retain a top consulting firm. Moreover, it worked. It started the process of bringing the company together."

In the early 1980s, highly visible business books like *Corporate Culture*, *In Search of Excellence*, and others championed the softer, more expressive side of corporate life. The key message: a tightly knit, well-focused, value-driven company culture pays handsome dividends over time. Since then, other authors have added impressive evidence to support the earlier claims.

★ John Kotter and James Haskett, in *Corporate Culture and Performance*, find that companies with cohesive, adaptive cultures geared to the business environment outperform comparison companies by a sizeable margin. They showed increased revenues by an average of 682 percent versus 166 percent, expanded workforces by 282 percent versus 36 percent, growth in stock prices by 901 percent versus 74 percent, and improved net incomes by 756 percent versus 1 percent.

★   James Collins and Jerry Porras, in *Built to Last: Successful Habits of Visionary Companies*, contrast three groups of companies: (1) visionary organizations whose core ideologies are woven tightly into their everyday practices; (2) good, above-average, but not great organizations; and (3) average stock market companies. They found striking differences in the growth of shareholder value among the three groups. Shareholders who in 1926 invested one dollar in the general stock market (average companies) would today have accumulated $415 in growth and dividends. Not bad. If that same dollar had been invested in a more select portfolio (above-average companies), shareholders today would have earned more than twice that amount, or $955. Even better. But wise investors whose 1926 dollar was placed in visionary companies would today see a portfolio worth $6,356.

★   Jeffrey Pfeffer, in *Competitive Advantage through People*, also illustrates how paying attention to the people-side of business reaps dividends. He finds that the top five performing stocks from 1972 through 1992 were as follows:

1. Southwest Airlines (return of 21,755 percent)

2. Wal-Mart Stores (19,807 percent)

3. Tyson Foods (18,118 percent)

4. Circuit City (16,410 percent)

5. Plenum Publishing (15,689 percent)

At least two of these companies—Southwest and Wal-Mart—are well known for their distinctive cultures and a healthy penchant for celebration.

★   In *America's Best: Industry Week's Guide to World-Class Manufacturing Plants*, Theodore Kinni reports that leaders of plants studied since 1990 reinforced the importance of paying attention to the people-side of business by building quality into processes, encouraging employee involvement, and developing community-building initiatives, all of which create structures for corporate citizenship. Investment in people and culture is necessary, he found, to create a world-class organization.

From this impressive evidence, a key maxim stands out: Results are driven by the crucial ingredients of culture and community—vision, relationships, and spirit. These give an enterprise substance, passion, and energy. According to Margaret Wheatley in *Leadership and the New Science*, nothing coheres a lifetime of activity more than meaning, and meaning always derives from a shared symbolic glue that bonds people together in a common quest. Ritual and ceremony, as prominent elements of culture along with vision and values, offer a major source for that glue. Without frequent ritual and ceremony, the symbolic ties that hold people together unravel; people split apart from each other, severing emotional ties with the company and losing their common hope, faith, and vision. As a result, the company loses its competitive edge, delivers a lackluster performance, and posts a dismal financial return.

Celebration as the Heart of Business

Ritual and ceremony undergird, interpenetrate, and intertwine with all aspects of corporate life: recognition, rewards, quality, teamwork, and leadership. Celebration is an integral element of culture and, as noted already, provides the symbolic adhesive that welds a community together. But there's more than that. Without transition ritual and ceremony, businesses cannot adjust to changing circumstances. In many different ways, celebration serves as an organization's heart. This is an alternative to the view that an organization's brain—information, analysis, and strategy—is the core.

This radical shift in thinking is akin to another conceptual revolution. Eons ago, people were certain that the sun and the other planets revolved around the earth. Ptolemaic theorists assured them that was the case. Conveniently, the facts always fit the theory. Later, Copernicus introduced a competing paradigm: The sun was the center of the solar system; the earth and the other planets revolved around the sun; and energy radiated from the sun. He accompanied his assertion with facts very difficult to ignore. For years Copernicus and the competing theorists argued and attacked one another. But Copernicus's theory prevailed. And even though Ptolemaic theory still aids us in navigation, its dominant influence on our thinking has receded.

Management theory, in some respects, is at a similar crossroad. We are locked in the throes of a major shift in worldviews or paradigms. For many years, we have assumed that the driving forces in business success are structure and strategy; they provide organizing energy. Everything else revolves around assumptions of rationality. Now we draw on a different conception: The epicenter of energy is a firm's purpose, vision, and values, the guiderails of culture. A primary expression of this cultural core is ritual and ceremony. These breathe spirit, passion, and purpose into everything else. In this view, everything revolves around celebration, the epicenter of a cultural system. (See figure 1.) This is not to say that structure and strategy are unimportant, but for a human organization to work well, we require the high-octane fuel, the spiritual juice, that meaningful ceremony provides.

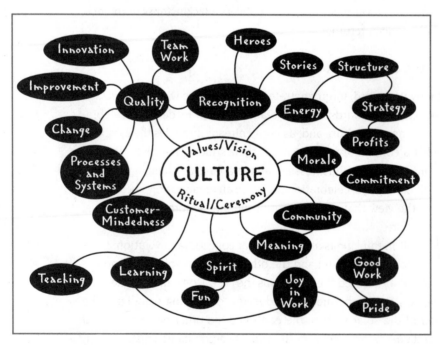

Figure 1. A Celebration-Centered View of Work

What's Holding Us Back?

Given compelling evidence and highly visible exemplars such as Southwest Airlines, Ben and Jerry's, Federal Express, Saturn, Wal-Mart, Nike, Starbucks, and Nordstrom, why don't more American companies sponsor high-caliber cultural celebrations? Rather than asking, Why should we? the real question should be, Why not? There are several critical barriers that block a shift in our thinking from a rationally dominated to a more spiritually centered view.

Discomfort

The first barrier is that many American executives and managers feel discomfort with the "softer" side of corporate life. They have been trained as financially oriented structural strategists, brought up to believe that rational is better, that restructuring and reengineering alone will lead to stronger performance. They tend to label what falls outside their rational purview as "touchy-feely." In fact, there is evidence that American managers may be the most left-brain dominant in the world, obsessed with a rational "control" paradigm. Charles Hampden-Turner, in *Creating Corporate Culture*, reports the results of a worldwide survey of managers' values. Among their international peers, U.S. managers rank highest in favoring rationality over more holistic approaches. A majority of U.S. managers accept profitability, or the bottom line, as the sole criterion of business success. By comparison, only 3 percent of Japanese managers share this belief. In Singapore, 89 percent reject the same premise that a majority of U.S. managers embrace.

Other research reveals corroborating evidence. A high percentage of U.S. managers favor rational logic over a symbolic view of organizations. (See Lee Bolman and Terrence Deal, "Leadership and Management Effectiveness.") It is no wonder, then, that in the United States, corporate celebrations often take a back seat to strategic planning and reengineering. Most American managers hang on to rational approaches and control tactics even though evidence exists to raise questions about their effectiveness.

Fear

A second barrier is related to the first. Many managers' discomfort with and distrust of symbols makes them unwilling to risk the chance that a celebration will backfire. In a way, their concerns are partially justified. Artificial, poorly timed, meaningless events are often worse than doing nothing. As one of our reviewers observed, "Meaningless work and artificial ceremony = meaningless work."

Scott Adams's *Dilbert* portrays the cynicism many feel when symbolic events are ill-timed or ill-suited to the prevailing situation. In a December 1996 comic strip, the office secretary informs Wally of his ten-year service anniversary. She invites him to pick a gift from the service anniversary catalog. He asks her if there will be a ceremony. She tells him that it has happened already. He asks if he can say a few words anyway. She responds, "Anywhere but here." Later, he mentions to Dilbert, his cubicle mate, that upon reviewing the catalog, he finds the ten-year awards somewhat meager. Dilbert, thumbing through the catalog, lets him know that the golf ball seems like a nice gift. But Wally is holding out for the "I'm with Stupid" T-shirt. Dilbert tells him that the catalog T-Shirt is blank. But upon closer inspection, Wally observes that it comes with a fabric pen. Dilbert then says, "I can almost feel the love our company has for us." Walking away, Wally says, "What do you mean us?"

Dilbert's satire, as usual, captures more truth than many of us would like to admit. Artificial celebrations are experienced either as a vacuous waste of time or another attempt to manipulate employees, to substitute frivolous frills for substantial rewards. Fear of having a celebration bomb or backfire keeps managers in a safer zone—play it safe or do nothing at all.

A real-life example of what managers fear actually did happen in the aftermath of the AT&T divestiture. An executive and his colleagues planned a sumptuous party to celebrate the newly formed company. The best of everything—food, wine, decorations, and accoutrements. It turned out to be the disaster of the year: poorly attended and poorly received by those who came. Afterward, employees wondered how the event's obvious costs could have enriched their own paychecks. They were feeling a sense of loss, grieving for the departure of Ma Bell and the Bell culture. The last thing they wanted was a high-priced festival to celebrate a less-than-widely embraced new beginning. No one wanted to dance on the grave of the old company.

Meaningless Events

In an attempt to rectify the situation, some managers move beyond their fears but unknowingly create a third barrier—repetitious, humdrum efforts to light a fire at work. Hosting hollow events is often worse than doing nothing at all. Following is one employee's description of a forced, superficial corporate celebration:

> I always dreaded corporate get-togethers. There was food and drink—nothing special—sometimes potluck, occasionally entertainment. More often there were boring speeches, which I listened to because they might have implications for my job, or there was a boring program. My only hope was to quickly find my buddies to hang out with. I guess what I really wanted was someone to hang on to. We would scan the scene looking for the higher-ups—some to pay our respects, others to route our escapes. People playing a predictable game. Tension in the air. Are we having fun yet? Not a chance. We got through it with a lingering aftertaste. Thank goodness it was over. At best it was painless: saw a few friends, had a few drinks. That's all.

The intention of management is often genuine; but the reaction of employees highlights the gap between what is intended and how it is interpreted or received.

Investor Resistance

Shareholders and external constituencies provide a fourth barrier to convening celebratory events. These ever-vigilant financial watchdogs are rightfully more concerned about their return on investment than the latest retreat to build morale and commitment. They want to see results, not hear secondhand about the price tag of the latest corporate "boondoggle." What they often fail to realize is that well-timed, well-orchestrated celebrations create the kind of spirit and energy that eventually pay off in terms of financial performance. But promises of long-term benefits often succumb to demands for quarterly accountability.

Separating Life and Work

A fifth barrier originates in our tendency to partition life and work. Life outside of the daily grind has its welcome parentheses, where we bracket special times away from repetitive routine: white spaces on which we paint life's deeper brush strokes. We experience these as individuals: the morning cup of coffee, walking the dog or letting the cat out at bedtime, shaving or putting on makeup. We also experience them with others: lunch breaks where we share food and languorous conversation, the late afternoon watering hole where we gather to ponder and to put into perspective the day's events. Our daily rituals are our modern liturgy to reflect and connect. As Robert Fulghum observes in his book, *From Beginning to End: The Rituals of Our Lives*, "Ritual allows us to experience the holy in the daily, the sacred in the single act of living" (p. 21).

Worldwide, seasonal occasions pep things up periodically and warm the hearts of even the most confirmed skeptics. There are autumn festivals such as Halloween, the Persian Mehregan, Yom Kippur, and Thanksgiving. Winter's cold weather and dark time pull us toward the hearth with ceremonies of candles, lights, fire, and hot toddies—Hanukkah, Christmas, Kwanzaa, and Shabyalda, a Persian winter feast. Spring's thaw spawns the Muslim New Year, Mardi Gras, Passover, Easter, Buddha's birthday, and St. Patrick's Day. Summer brings picnics, outings, and sports events. But more often than not, these special occasions are experienced outside the workplace. The job is something to get away from, not to make an integral part of life. We lose ourselves on the job only to recover our humanity once we return home. Maybe that's why more heart attacks are reported to occur on Monday mornings between the hours of seven and nine than at any other time.

We live—that is, really live—at home; we tend to merely exist in the weekday drudgery on the job. As a result, a significant chunk of our lives is sacrificed in a sterile, spiritless workplace. That's a waste that should not prevail. As James Autry reminds us in *Life and Work*:

> Most managers and their companies also affirm that people dislike working and, given the chance, would walk away from it. By assuming that people really don't want to work, we establish rules, policies, and procedures that serve to restrict rather than enable or empower people (p. 15).

Lack of Know-How

This final barrier—managers don't always know how to convene authentic, meaningful occasions—is the primary subject of this book. Symbolic issues rarely receive the attention commanded by structure and strategy in management education. As a result, managers often lack the symbolic knowledge that leaders must have to be effective. Yet symbols are the stuff of good leadership. In *Organizational Culture and Leadership*, Edgar Schein reminds us of the possibility "that the only thing of real importance leaders do is to create and manage culture and that the unique ability of leaders is their ability to work with culture" (p. 2).

> **Festivity, like play, contemplation, and making love, is an end in itself. It is not instrumental.**
>
> —Harvey Cox, *Feast of Fools*

The literature on leadership today is calling for systems thinkers, servant leaders/stewards, visionaries, coaches/mentors, change managers, teachers/learners, shapers of meaning and culture. At the core of leadership, in our current view, is the ability to create and encourage celebration. If you don't feel comfortable with or know how to foster celebration, there is a leadership shortfall, particularly since ritual and ceremony play such an influential role in culture maintenance, reinforcement, and transformation. Celebration is not an add-on; it is the center source, the spiritual fuel that ignites performance and propels a culture forward.

How to Use This Book

To aid leaders (and managers) in creating meaningful corporate events, this book is organized into three main sections. Part 1 (which incorporates this chapter) lays the foundation. It outlines why celebration is potentially such a big topic and builds a case for ritual and ceremony at work. Chapter 2 highlights the individual and group benefits that ritual and ceremony offer in the workplace and sketches the variety of occasions where ritual and ceremony play a vital role.

Part 2 describes in more detail the various forms that ritual and ceremony assume: marking cyclical milestones, acknowledging and recognizing individual and group contributions, exalting in triumphs and successes, coping with calamity and loss, dealing with entrances and exits, getting together to do good deeds for others, and encouraging play for its own sake. This section features examples from high-performing companies, not as recipes to be followed but as exemplars to stimulate creative thinking.

Part 3 outlines "how-to" principles for convening meaningful events: setting the stage, orchestrating the details, improvising where necessary, assuring fond memories that last beyond the event, and highlighting the role of key players. As thought interruption, we offer some tongue-in-cheek suggestions for killing an event—assuring that nothing exciting, meaningful, or memorable will happen. The concluding chapter reemphasizes the importance of reviving joy and spirit in the modern workplace, summing it up with some guiding principles. We hope, in the end, to have imparted to you, the reader, the power of ritual and ceremony and, even more important, the permission to celebrate. In doing so, we create new possibilities for making more noble workplaces, enhancing America's global ability to compete, and stoking a more robust financial performance.

Chapter 2

What Makes an Effective Celebration?

The procession began. All stood in honor of the occasion and turned to watch the parade from the narthex of the church. Before any person appeared, the distant bagpipes began to wail a sad hymn. As they grew louder and closer, we could hear a growing rattle, drumsticks riveting on the rim of the snares. The music crescendoed as the organ pined the hum and rattle. Our hearts began to swell, and tears pressed to be released. So beautiful were the people in their costumes, the family plaids and tartans, as they walked proudly through the center aisle, gathered in their clans. And then one young couple came into view—the very image of wild and free. Both were dressed in authentic, historic garb: she in a full-length ivory gown, hair plaited in knots and ribbons; he in a long coat over his kilt and stockings, with shocks of blond wavy hair and one gold earring.

They held their heads high and smiled slightly. The music continued to swell, and the room filled with emotion. We could hardly breathe for the majesty of it all.

As all were seated and quiet fell, the minister began to tell stories of the Scottish people and their heritage. How the Scots were known for inventing golf but less known for being the first to mandate education for every girl and boy, rich and poor, and also the first to ordain laity into their formal church administration. After the British defeated the Scots again in 1746, they outlawed church activities; display of family colors, tartans, or kilts; and the playing of Scottish music in an attempt to defeat the traditional culture. These were considered instruments of war. To survive and keep shared ways alive, people hid a tiny piece of family cloth in their pockets and took it out to be blessed during clandestine ceremonies, secretly held in Kirks, their church-schools. After the telling of stories, the procession withdrew, to the bagpipes playing "Amazing Grace" and, again, the incredible rattle of the snares. Even at this writing and after some twenty tellings, I cannot suppress the tears; nor can the listeners I have told.

This ceremony, "Kirkin' (or Churchin') of the Tartans," was revived by Peter Marshall during World War II, when Nazi Germany was terrorizing free people. It is now held annually in some sectors of the Presbyterian faith in the United States. It matters little whether you are Scottish, Presbyterian, or even Christian. There is a fundamental power in this traditional ceremony that stirs the psyche and kindles deep emotions. It brings up core values—freedom, family, faith, fairness. Pride exudes for whomever can let the ceremony's spirit overcome adversity and embrace what is good about life and humanity. What are the attributes that make this celebration so powerful?

Universal Attributes of Celebration

The following components, which build the poignant experience of the Kirkin' of the Tartans, reveal the universal ingredients of meaningful ceremonies:

★ Powerful *music*, both in the quality of the sound and the choice of songs.

★ The *rattle, drums, and bells*, primitive connections to the heart.

★ *Stylized behavior*—parade, dance, procession done to the cadence of the *occasion*; a march creating observation of what and who is honored.

★ *Costumes* and *symbols*, such as flags and colors, connoting family and affiliation.

★ *Storytelling* to convey the voyage and victory of a people to preserve their cherished *values*.

★ Order in the *structure* of the ritual, with spontaneous artistry on the part of the costume designers and those in costume.

★ The *aesthetics* of flowers, smells, and sounds.

★ A sacred space where all have a chance to *participate* as a *community*—speak, sing, and privately relate to their faith and higher purpose.

Celebration is vital to the human psyche. All of us have an emotional craving, a deep-seated need to participate in ritual and ceremony. When we do, each of us experiences extraordinary intrapsychic feelings. Most everyone can recall a celebration where he or she felt truly significant, important, full of emotion and meaning. Not only that, most everyone can readily step back after an event and identify the attributes of an authentic celebration. All of us have such memories: a Boy or Girl Scout achievement; a sports team rally in the auditorium and a victory; a patriotic song on the Fourth of July; the march on Washington led by Martin Luther King, Jr.; touching the Vietnam Memorial on Memorial Day; singing "America the Beautiful" with a group; or playing a funeral dirge for a friend. Our chests swell with palpable feeling connecting us to our inner selves, to others, and to the enduring human spirit.

The *Me-We* Connection

In an authentic celebration, people are willing to step out of their daily routine, drop their outer masks, and be fully present in the occasion: being a *part* (we) and also being *apart* (me). In the experience of *we* is the collective sense of family, inclusiveness, communion, belonging, connection, solidarity, a common purpose, vision, and values. We cannot be complete as individuals unless we are deeply involved in community, and there can't be a community without unique individuals. In addition to coalescing a community, celebration cultivates feelings of being valued for oneself, heightens self-esteem, and encourages freedom of genuine expression—fun, humor, and the creative aspects of life. In celebration, the *me* joins the *we*.

      Apart   **The Individual**

A part   **The Connected**

Notice the mirror effect of *me* and *we*; if we place one on top of the other, the letters *m* and *w* are reverse images.

People simultaneously want both—to be apart, *me*, and to be a part, *we*. In celebration, the mirror images of *me* and *we* interplay and fuse as one, inviting unself-conscious participation that eliminates fear, satisfies basic psychological needs, and connects everyone in the creative flow of true community.

The Qualities of Effective Celebrations

The qualities that give celebrations special status are not the guarded secrets of cultural experts; they are widely known. People can readily identify the functional attributes of authentic, meaningful celebrations—bonding, a sense of shared purpose, and a common spirit. In several social experiments, we asked a variety of executives and professionals to identify the ingredients of "a really great celebration." After putting each identified quality on a Post-it™, groups of fifteen to twenty people met at a wall of flip-chart paper to cluster like items in an affinity diagram. Over and over again, group after group, the same aggregates appeared.

The largest clusters always occurred around certain key ideas: people, purpose, joy/fun, place, music, and food. There would be a small cluster devoted to planning, dollars, and a director of the event—some leadership to pull it off. And one single Post-it™ promoted the idea of "celebration as a lifelong experience." In this experiment, we observed a transition from clusters that emphasize individual feelings—the *me* experiences—to clusters that highlight collective experiences—the affiliation and common focus of *we*. The happy combined result is an individual high as well as a coming together of people in a spirit of connectedness and higher purpose. Following are the clusters that our experiments revealed.

Feelings Abound

The predominant theme of this cluster is joy. There are ideas of energy, an element of surprise and amazement, and the presence of gratitude. Meaningful celebration is full of feelings. Some of those feelings are intrapsychic, but many are in relation to others. They are feelings freed by the conditions described in the next cluster, which create an environment where people can be themselves without fear.

People Feel Free and Uninhibited

W. Edwards Deming, the quality leader whose ideas we draw on frequently, saw fear as a major predator of joy in work. People reveal themselves in festival. Disinhibitions drive out fear. Thereafter, participation flows more freely. Humor is a universal disinhibitor. Laughter is the ally of optimism, shifting people from grousing and griping to a more positive state of conviviality and joy. There is tremendous release in uninhibited expression of emotion without fear of judgment or reprisal. For Deming, toxic and competitive systems of grading, ranking,

rating, punishment—even overre-warding people—rob the work-place of emotional buoyancy. Surprise, joy, amazement, and enthusiasm are emotions associated with creative energy—the antithesis of fear.

Accoutrements of Fun Appear

Many modern adults are starved for play. Fun is pure process, full expression, an end in itself. It is the antithesis of competition—to win or score points. Great

celebrations provide a temporary license for fun, excess, and abandonment. People live it up. They eat too much, occasionally drink too much, and often stay out too late. Skits, games, sports, and festivals encourage unself-conscious play. In fantasy-like abandonment, individuals become unconstrained by rules, policy, status, or limits. People experience the joy of letting go. Often when people put on costumes, they disarm themselves. Something other than their outer masks of personality take over, and they reveal their creative, expressive selves—they experience true freedom.

People are quick to point out what makes a party—food and music, decorations, a great location, entertainment. Note the sensory aspects (smells, feel of the room, weather) and the idea of capturing memories in pictures. These are components of party-making that symbolize celebration to people.

Family and Affiliation: The Collective Experience

Affiliation is a means of survival in our species. It is also the underpinning of self-esteem—you are honored and affirmed by being accepted and belonging to a cohesive group.

Celebrations feature inclusiveness: I belong to a family, a team, other people. Celebrations help build interpersonal union by fostering common roots and traditions. They provide social support for being yourself and believing that you matter, that your talents are appreciated and used. Ritual and ceremony acculturate, give meaning to symbols, and help people learn a common language. Peter Block, in his book *Stewardship*, sees a vital need for personal connectedness in the workplace because the workplace has become the era's new ecumenical cathedral, one of the few

places where people congregate anymore. Marianne Williamson, in *A Return to Love*, also sees the workplace as a front for a temple, a healing place for people. Celebration knits individual psyches into a shared feeling of fellowship and family.

Focus: Every Function Has a Functional Payoff

Without a common vision or purpose, individual effort fragments into a grating cacophony rather than a pleasurable symphony. The result is dangling discord, with almost everyone singing from a different song sheet or following his or her unique script. Celebration needs to have a focal point, a reason, a theme, which

becomes the framework for expression. What we do for the sheer joy of it also helps an organization function at a higher level of performance—something we too often forget or ignore. Celebration creates and focuses the energy needed for an organization to produce results.

Business Benefits of Special Occasions

As our groups of executives and professionals also pointed out, too often celebrations are thought of as purely expressive events—festive ends in themselves. We participate in celebrations for the joy they offer and what they reveal to us of life's deeper mysteries and meaning. At the same time, especially in the workplace, ritual and ceremony have functional consequences. They address issues that otherwise interfere with an organization's ability to accomplish important goals and objectives. To summarize, generic functions of celebrations include

★ building relationships among individuals, strengthening bonds across diverse subcultures, and knitting the community together;

★ leveling the hierarchy to provide a common ground where bosses, managers, and employees can intermingle freely without fear;

★ summoning the collective spirit, which creates energy, excitement, commitment, and loyalty;

★ establishing a connection between historical roots, current realities, and future dreams;

★ allowing intangible values and visions to be experienced and appreciated;

★ transforming difficulties into opportunities, tragedies into growth experiences, losses into gains;

★ providing access to life's deeper lessons and creating true learning organizations;

★ providing a safety valve to discharge drives, relieve tension, express emotion, and deal with conflict;

★ creating a forum for sharing stories, breaking bread, dancing, and linking joy with work.

In our view, the shortfall between an optimistic strategic forecast and a less-than-robust financial performance has two main causes: (1) individuals who are unhappy, unmotivated, and dissatisfied; and (2) an organization that relies mainly on short-term, rationally based management strategies to focus energy and produce results. Celebration helps narrow the performance gap by simultaneously stimulating positive feelings and knitting people together in a well-focused, unified work community.

Forms of Celebration

Timing is crucial to staging an effective celebration. Different feelings and functions emerge as ritual and ceremony take unique forms at different times: cyclical celebrations, recognition ceremonies, celebrations of triumph, rituals of comfort and letting go for gatherings at times of chaos or calamity, succession rites, altruistic celebrations, and play. Table 1 links celebratory forms to individual feelings and collective functions.

FORMS	FEELINGS	FUNCTIONS
Cyclical Celebrations	Identity Inner rhythm	Provide external sanction for internal bonding
Recognition Ceremonies	Self-esteem Motivation Awareness	Convey shared values Create cultural heroes and heroines Focus energy and provide motivation
Celebrations of Triumph	Joy Hope Affiliation	Create energy Connect individual efforts with collective success Spawn stories Provide symbolic glue
Comfort and Letting Go	Grief Sadness Hope	Heal collective wounds Help group move on Create a sense of continuity among past, present, and future
Succession Rites	Closure Emotion Letting go	Help departing people move on Help surviving people let go Help replacements ease in Reaffirm continuity Reinforce shared values
Altruistic Celebrations	Love Charity Altruism	Pull people together Give something back to the community Recognize customers and other external players
Play	Delight Surprise Release	Release tension Foster creativity and new initiatives Bond a group together

Table 1. Forms, Feelings, and Functions of Celebration

Cyclical Celebrations

Seasonal events draw on recurring seasonal themes or key milestones in a company's history. In every culture, the changing of the seasons sparks some kind of ceremonial recognition. Within an organization, corporate anniversaries or individual birthdays create a welcome excuse for festive ceremonies or rituals. Cyclical events create an endless spiral that knits past, present, and future into a meaningful workplace tapestry.

Recognition Ceremonies

Recognition events generate public applause in appreciation for special accomplishments and extraordinary deeds deserving of everyone's attention. Such occasions anoint heroes and heroines, living logos who exemplify core values and beliefs. Recognition for a job well done yields motivation for noble efforts yet to come.

Celebrations of Triumph

Occasions to celebrate high points create energy at times of success. They dramatize the link between the hard work of individuals and the stellar performance of the group as a whole. The high-five adrenaline release of winning welds diversity into unity, however disparate the workforce.

Rituals of Comfort and Letting Go

Not all times are good times: Life in organizations produces calamity and loss in proportion to success and gain. Ritual and ceremony generate hope and faith when things are going poorly or bottoming out. Just as winning can draw people together, so too can life's darkest moments. Change, for example, produces as much pain as gain. It is like a trapeze act—people have to let go of old traditions before they can latch on to new ways. The timing of when to let go in order to catch the new momentum is crucial to a successful performance. As old ways or practices die out, they leave collective wounds or losses that only ritual can effectively begin to heal.

Succession Rites

As individuals come and go, transition events help organizations cope and regroup. Managers and employees enter and exit all the time, voiding relationships essential to teamwork and cooperation. Transition rituals serve three important functions: (1) they help departing people sever ties, put the past into perspective, and reattach themselves to new circumstances; (2) they help those who remain let go and move on without warm memories being eclipsed by debilitating pain; and (3) they ease the entrance of replacements, allowing members to establish themselves in a new situation without their efforts being canceled out by old obligations.

Altruistic Celebrations

Celebrations that benefit others outside the corporate family provide opportunities to say thank you to economic partners—customers or clients—as well as a chance for everyone to pull together in giving something back to the local community. Doing for others helps to solidify individuals as a cohesive group.

Play for Play's Sake

Play is the wellspring of creativity, the universal language. It's one of the best ways to infuse the workplace with both the juice that creates energy and the glue that cements relationships. People who play together tend to stay together, linked through frolic and fun—an idea promoted by Matt Weinstein, CEO of Playfair and author of the book *Managing to Have Fun*.

Effective Celebration: Emotions, Functions, and Forms

Individuals come to work as much for meaning as for money. Ritual and ceremony are too often ignored as effective ways to infuse the workplace with energy and meaning. It is not difficult to find reasons for celebrations; it can be more difficult, however, to figure out how to imbue celebrations with all the important pay-offs—feeling, freedom, affiliation, fun—and to choose an authentic and well-timed focus.

Celebrations have feelings, functions, and forms that go with them. Call the overall experience *soul*, a mood that cannot be manufactured. It is, in its essence, spirit. Something to be summoned, called up, as it lies waiting beneath the surface of our being. We can give it a place to emerge, but we cannot create it; we can only call it forth. We give it context; it paints the design. It is the creative space that gives life meaning and majesty.

In the following chapters, we explore in more depth different types of celebrations, demonstrating through examples how many companies are sponsoring symbolic events in order to reap their psychological and functional benefits.

> **The vernacular sources of soul in society . . . food, celebration, relationships . . . the world of particulars.**
>
> —Thomas Moore, *SoulMates*

PART TWO

Forms and Uses of Celebration

Chapter 3

Marking Milestones: Cyclical Celebrations

Life evolves in cycles. As individuals, we experience birth, growth, maturity, and ultimately death. As employees or managers, we see organizations arise, grow, and sometimes stagnate or die. Each year we witness the new start of spring, the

> **To everything,**
> **Turn . . . turn . . . turn,**
> **There is a season,**
> **Turn . . . turn . . . turn.**
>
> **And a time to every purpose**
> **Under heaven.**
>
> —Ecclesiastes 3:1,
> as sung by The Byrds

vagaries of summer, the bounty and decline of autumn, and winter's stillness and darkness. Somewhere in the evolution of the human species, our ancestors—probably through trial and error—stumbled on a vital lesson: We need to stop once in a while to acknowledge the passage of time. Our genetic makeup and cultural heritage tell us that without periodic pauses interspersed among life's recurring cycles, we lose our bearings. We become deprived of a vital sense of how

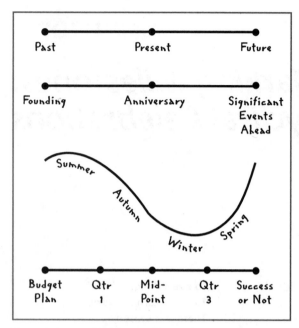

Past   Present   Future

Founding   Anniversary   Significant
                               Events
                               Ahead

Summer
Autumn
Winter   Spring

Budget   Qtr   Mid-   Qtr   Success
Plan   1   Point   3   or Not

Figure 2. Forms of Celebration That Cycle

past, present, and future weave together in a meaningful package. (See figure 2.)

Thankfully, most people are aware of the existential vacuum that timeless humdrum and repetition can create. As a result, they strive to punctuate life's cycles with periodic pauses. Well-intentioned seasonal events can miss the mark, however. For example, a television station in one city planned its annual summer picnic at the local amusement park. Instead of making it a group event, employees were given tickets and told to use them anytime, although one day had been set aside as the official "Channel 13 Day." As a result, employees trickled into the park in individual family units—not exactly a cohesive, focused gathering— and nothing was offered to help people come together. A memo was sent out trying to explain and correct the confusion, but it did little to bring some shared oomph to the occasion.

Many contemporary leaders are equally sensitive to the importance of marking important milestones. Properly planned, these are rarely repetitious, mindless occasions; they are secularly inspired efforts to give the cycle of life special meaning. Some of the ways companies do this are by (1) acknowledging individual birthdays, (2) recognizing corporate anniversaries, (3) convening special occasions around the seasons, and (4) infusing once-a-year fiscal reviews with a celebratory flair. Each practice provides an opportunity to spice up routine, celebrate progress, and create transitions between seasons and stages.

Acknowledging Individual Birthdays

In many organizations, the only regular gathering for people to celebrate the passage of time arises around peoples' birthdays. Usually held at the local office level, birthday celebrations give people a brief break from the daily grind: going to lunch together, sharing some cake, having a beer, or doing something else special.

In a recent visit to a large insurance company, we were having lunch with top executives in the presidential dining room when all of a sudden the electrical power in the headquarters went off. We all sat silently in the dark for a few moments. Then came the sounds of people singing "Happy Birthday." We made our way down the hall and there, bathed in candlelight, were the songsters. The company's legal staff was celebrating the birthday of one of the senior legal secretaries. We connected to the festivities. The camaraderie, candlelight, champagne, and group spirit made us all forget the power outage. To some managers, a brief interlude like this may smack of superficiality or fluff. But when people are part of a meaningful, authentic event, it is easy to get caught up in the celebratory spirit. Birthday parties can become a legitimate excuse to have a little fun on the job.

Some birthday activities, such as those described below, become more sophisticated collective rites of passage.

> I don't know how it started, but we took to taping across everyone's door on their birthday—it was a sign of impending disaster inside the person's office. Whatever was the known passion of the person, we took it to excess. One liked M&Ms; we filled his office full. They were in his briefcase, in his drawers, and scattered all over the place. Another liked flowers—petals everywhere. We all kept an eye peeled for the birthday person's arrival and as they showed up, shouted "Surprise," calibrating their reaction through every phase of getting their office back together. We had a lot of fun with this.

The annual birthday event does not always have to be marked with such gala attention. It can be recognized with a simple, symbolic gesture such as a card or a present. In one Equicor office, a flip-chart easel was hid out of the birthday person's view. Then everyone took a secret turn answering the question at the top of the page: "The thing I like most about (name) is _____." After everyone filled the giant flip-chart "card" with remarks, it was presented to the associate on his or her big day. Most people left their card taped up on their door for quite a long time.

And finally, in 1001 *Ways to Reward Employees*, Bob Nelson describes how the Veterans Administration Philadelphia Regional Office and Insurance Center celebrates birthdays. Employees are allowed to grant an Extra Step Award to coworkers during the month of the coworkers' birthdays. They are awarded cash prizes of $30 for going out of their way to delight their internal customers.

Across these examples, the underlying theme is the same: Birthdays are special occasions. They provide a legitimate excuse to stop for awhile and share something all people have in common. Particularly when a workplace offers little else in the way of celebration, birthdays offer at least a temporary feeling of friendship and family. Too often these moments provide the only bonds that hold people together in a shared enterprise.

Recognizing Anniversaries

Both individuals and companies have anniversaries that can be celebrated. Anniversaries of both kinds provide an opportunity to rekindle the spirit of the birth of a relationship, to reconnect people with what they hold most dear, and to recommit everyone to the goals waiting to be accomplished in the years ahead.

Personal Anniversaries

The day of one's birth is not the only personal milestone observed at work. Many businesses also salute a predetermined number of years someone has served with the company, and these annual occasions provide another opportunity to draw people together. Recognizing years of service marks an important milestone and offers another special moment as well—an opportunity to reinforce company values.

Again in 1001 *Ways to Reward Employees*, Bob Nelson gives an example of such a company practice. Wilson Learning Corporation of Minnesota, a training and development firm, gives employees Mickey Mouse watches after their first three months as a reminder to have fun on the job. On their tenth anniversaries, they receive gold Mickey Mouse watches.

Some executives go out of their way to acknowledge those employees who have been with the company for an extended length of time. Max DePree, CEO of Herman Miller and well-known business author, hosted a corporate-wide event in the fall of 1987, recognizing four hundred of the company's employees who had twenty or more years of service. The celebration was held at the company's headquarters and videotaped. The symbolic focal point was the unveiling of an abstract sculpture entitled *The Tribal Water Carrier*. DePree explained the statue's significance to the assembled crowd by drawing an analogy between tribal life and life in a modern corporation. In tribes, he explained, the water carrier had the most important job because water, like air and food, is essential to survival. The modern corporation depends just as heavily on vitality, renewal, continuity, and life-giving commitment. "To be a [contemporary] water carrier means involving yourself in the transfer of the company culture and values to new people who arrive on the scene to help us and then they eventually replace us," DePree said.

After DePree defined the sculpture's significance, he announced that a miniature version would stand inside the headquarters. It would sit next to the CEO's office symbolizing the moral responsibility of company elders to pass on the Herman Miller history, values, and culture. According to DePree, "The sculpture is a reminder of people who have invested their life in a significant way."

After the dedication ceremony, honorees gathered around the artwork to see and touch their names, which had been inscribed in the circular granite base. Herman Miller uses celebration of longtime individual service to convey the company's long-standing cultural traditions. Always well attended, the ceremonies draw out stories and memories that connect generations of employees in a meaningful union. Old-timers receive due recognition while newcomers begin to learn the ropes, understand why the company's heroes and heroines are revered, and see how they too will eventually shape the future of the company.

Corporate Anniversaries

Annual observances of Founder's Day or whatever label is attached to such an event provide a yearly chance to gather people together and revisit traditional roots. Of special significance are anniversaries of five, ten, twenty, twenty-five, and so forth years.

Anderson Soft-Teach, a Silicon Valley software firm, celebrated ten years in business by taking all forty employees (plus spouses) to Hawaii. The generosity of Warren E. Anderson, the company's founder, motivated employees to do their part to make the event truly memorable.

★ One employee scanned a picture of Anderson and gave him a James Brown hairdo. The image was printed on false currency called "Warren Bucks" that was redeemable for drinks at the opening evening's festivities.

★ Three employees met before the trip and wrote a song for the occasion. They gathered everyone together to rehearse, and surprised Anderson by singing the song on the first evening. A full moon rose after sunset to top off the occasion.

Anderson commented on the benefits of the event:

Well, it sure was easy to hire new employees for the four months prior to the trip. But seriously, we created a company legend complete with lots of stories that are still repeated to this day, especially to new employees not here for the trip. And it illustrated our system of values and beliefs far better than anything else I could have done.

Southwest Airlines, top of the line as far as festive, fun-driven companies go, shows how a company's twentieth birthday can be celebrated with style. The gala event was held in a tastefully decorated hangar in Austin, Texas, the company's birthplace. It was attended by employees, politicians, and longtime friends. Pride and patriotism reigned supreme as outside celebrities, such as singers and dancers from the Texas Incredible Productions Company, the Kilgore (Texas) Rangerettes, and emcee singer and songwriter Rod Steagall, delighted the crowd during dinner. After dinner, the Gatlin Brothers performed for an hour. Even more important, the event showcased the company's own local talent. During the sumptuous dinner, photographs of Southwest employees and reruns of some of its most successful commercials put the company's spirit on display. Southwest's regional director of ground operations, himself a state fiddle champion, brought the crowd to its feet with a stirring rendition of "Orange Blossom Special." The LUV Notes, a group of women from two of Southwest's departments, brought the house down singing their own version of Billy Joel's "We Didn't Start the Fire." Their original lyrics highlighted major events in Southwest's first twenty years. After the Gatlin Brothers' performance, Herb Kelleher, CEO of Southwest, thanked the crowd for their role in hanging in there with the company over the years.

Kevin and Jackie Freiberg, in their book about Southwest Airlines, NUTS: *Southwest Airlines Crazy Recipe for Business and Personal Success*, described the grand finale as follows:

After his heartfelt speech, Kelleher invited the Gatlin Brothers back to sing one final song. Joined by a cadre of Southwest employees, the Rangerettes, and Incredible Productions, the Gatlins belted out "The Lone Star Is Flying High," written by Tim McClure of GSD&M especially for the occasion to commemorate the goodwill Southwest had built in the heartland of Texas. It was a grand finale that rivaled the close of the Grammies (pp. 175–76).

The celebratory spirit marking anniversaries is contagious across Southwest's airport operations. To recognize its tenth year in Nashville, for example, a local station staged a ceremony scripted to the number ten, which is described by Diane Cox, marketing coordinator at Southwest Airlines.

We brought in ten chefs at ten o'clock in the morning to do a ten-minute cake decorating contest using ten ingredients. The contest was judged by ten year olds. It was a lot of fun because it was a multigenerational event. Everybody in the airport was excited. It was just like a birthday party. It had the feeling of excitement you had as a child.

Anderson Soft-Teach and Southwest Airlines are not alone in the special attention given to anniversaries. Other companies are moving away from potentially stodgy Founder's Day events to sponsor upbeat annual get-togethers commensurate with core values.

Celebrations in Lean Years

It's relatively easy to recognize anniversaries that fall in prosperous years, but what to do when the date rolls around and things are less than prosperous? Some companies dutifully celebrate important historical milestones, even when current performance is off the mark.

For example, a large financial company was nearing its twenty-fifth year in business. The problem was that the company's performance in its quarter-century year was less than robust. This created a dilemma for the CEO. Should he just let the anniversary slip by without special recognition? The decision was to go all out in a tasteful way. A black-tie dinner for all employees featured an evening of memories and a powerful, emotional speech from the president letting everyone know that the company's roots were deep and strong and "together we will make the next twenty-five years even more spectacular than the first twenty-five." A standing ovation let the executive know that he'd made the right decision. The company's next year's performance reinforced his on-the-spot conclusion.

Sponsoring Seasonal Festivities

Each year provides seasonal opportunities for marking time: summer picnics, Halloween, Thanksgiving, winter parties, spring holidays. Authentic, meaningful seasonal celebrations are important to employees. They provide periodic occasions to mingle, munch, and quaff with colleagues in an informal, festive atmosphere. Informality also reduces the hierarchical distance between managers and employees, giving people at both levels a chance to meet on common ground.

One company, Spectrum Healthcare Services in St. Louis, Missouri, tries to celebrate each holiday in a special way. Following are some of their ideas, taken from Barbara Glanz's book, *Care Packages*:

★ A "You Are Loved" pin on every employee's desk on Valentine's Day.

★ Green popcorn on St. Patrick's Day.

★ On Easter, a display of baby pictures of the executives and a contest to identify which baby is now a big shot.

★ Low-fat frozen yogurt on the Fourth of July to capture the spirit of the day and reinforce the importance of employee health.

★ Costume and pumpkin-carving contests on Halloween.

★ A potluck at Thanksgiving, with each employee bringing a favorite dish.

★ Holiday parties in December.

★ Three helium balloons on each employee's birthday.

★ File clean-out days twice a year, with casual dress (pp. 190–91).

While such gestures may seem trivial to outsiders, within a company meaningful events interspersed to coincide with special seasons can have a significant impact on morale, motivation, and commitment.

Many companies use society's holidays to convene people in gatherings that may not even coincide with the yearly calendar. An off-time seasonal event can gain even more unique meaning within a company. Southwest Airlines, again, provides a state-of-the-art example, which capitalizes on seasonal rhythms even as the company's growth makes in-sync celebrations hard to pull off. Following is a description by Kevin and Jackie Freiberg:

> When the system grew so large that it was impossible to have just one Christmas party, Southwest decided to throw three company parties. When having all the Christmas parties during December got to be just a bit overwhelming, with all the other year-end activities facing Southwest employees, Colleen Barrett (senior vice president) simply decided to hold them at different times of the year. Can you imagine a Christmas party in July? That's what happened in Oakland. Christmas in September? That's what they had in Chicago. At least a thousand employees turned out for an enjoyable evening of Christmas carols and merriment in each location. The parties were such a success that the company plans to keep on having them at oddball times (p. 184).

Sometimes sales quotas, project deadlines, or the push for production and profit can make it hard to set aside time for seasonal celebrations. At H. B. Fuller, an international producer of industrial adhesives based in Minneapolis–St. Paul, Minnesota, and a company widely recognized for its solid ethics and sensitive attention to its corporate culture, employees at one of the glue-making operations look forward to the annual holiday party as one of the year's high points. They and their spouses go to great lengths to dress up for the occasion. The plant manager says, "It's the one time during the year we can let our hair down and enjoy one another. We eat, drink, dance, and tell stories. We remember those who are no longer with us. We join together in wishing for more prosperous times ahead."

During the holidays a number of years ago, the plant was operating at full capacity, twenty-four hours a day, seven days a week. The intense, rapid pace was an economic necessity in order to keep abreast of customer demand for adhesive products. The question was what to do about the holiday party. To honor tradition meant idling the plant for at least two shifts—an expensive and time-consuming proposition. The problem was solved when several of the company's retirees volunteered to staff the manufacturing operation for evening and graveyard shifts so the event could go on as scheduled. The old-timers enjoyed the opportunity to get back into harness. The current employees renewed relationships at their annual festival. Later, the employees hosted a party for the retirees to thank them for their thoughtfulness and generosity.

Invigorating Annual Performance Reviews

The annual corporate financial review can be a somber event—reams and recitations of facts and figures can dominate feelings of festival and fun. Not so at NRDC, a Nashville-based telephone repair division of Nortel. Its annual review is a companywide event attended by all employees, who are given the day off to be there. Successes and issues in all parts of the business are made public and discussed openly. This gives everyone the big picture as well as insight into their own contribution to the overall performance.

In another company, a large food-distribution enterprise, managers meet off-site each year to review the company's financial performance. Bottom-line results are typically presented on an overhead projector in a straightforward, cut-and-dry fashion in a late afternoon session. Because the results are shown for each operation, there is typically a lot of anxiety before the review session and, depending on the results, a great deal of gloating or excuse-making afterwards. One year, the CEO unexpectedly altered the format. An eyewitness described the dramatic results.

> We were all dressed up in suits and ties—just like always. We sat down and awaited the traditional facts and figures about our year's financial performance. The president got up, and rather than turning on the overhead, started to talk about the founding of the company. The founder, as always, was in his seat toward the back of the room. Shows up every year. As the president recalled the story, tears started rolling down the founder's face. Then came audible sobs. Pretty soon, nearly everyone was in

tears—a very emotional time. Then the president turned to the financial report with a caution: "But let's never forget who we are or how we got here. It's what we stand for that makes our bottom line. Always has been. Always will be."

The Seasonal Flow of Celebrations

Properly planned and carried out, cyclical celebrations contribute predictable, welcome, and poignant pulse points in the organization's life cycle. Marking milestones builds historical continuity and a communal collection of cherished memories. Individual birthdays and corporate anniversaries help set the stage for meetings that matter. The seasonal flow of life outside work spawns energy and spirit that can be pulled inside to give zest and buoyancy to corporate occasions. Without symbolic markers in the passage of time, life and work become a dreary and endless series of Wednesdays. Breaking the cycle with meaningful ritual and ceremony infuses the workplace with zest, zeal, and passion. In the parade of time, symbolic parentheses draw up the human spirit.

Chapter 4

Acknowledgment and Recognition: Celebrating Individual and Team Performance

n more recent times, W. Edwards Deming underscored William James's timeless maxim as a surefire assurance of high quality: "Everyone counts."

> **The deepest principle in human nature is the craving to be appreciated.**
>
> —William James

Any small short circuit in an organization's production process can jeopardize quality standards. One person's shoddy contribution can undercut the overall worth of a product or service. All it takes is one. Each person adds or subtracts value with his or her work. Each has gifts; management's challenge is to find them and invite them to the table. What gives people incentive to do their best? People are naturally motivated when individual contributions are recognized and appreciated. This innate need for appreciation is not a selfish, superficial craving for the center spotlight; it is an authentic, deep-seated desire to be deemed as worthy when offering something of worth.

People do not work for praise, but they do enjoy the feeling of being valued and appreciated. In a study of fifteen hundred employees reported by Bob Nelson in 1001 *Ways to Reward Employees*, personal congratulations by managers ranked first out of sixty-seven potential sought-after incentives. Another study reported by Barbara Glanz in *Care Packages* shows that executives seem to agree with employees on the issue. Thirty-four percent of 150 executives interviewed saw limited recognition and praise as one of the most common reasons why employees leave the workplace. Recognition ranks ahead of salary and other motivators.

From a coworker's simple compliment to elaborate recognition ceremonies embellished with certificates, prizes, and awards, the ritualistic "thank you" is one of the work world's most common expressive events. As with all ritual and ceremony, there is an implicit subtext. On the surface, the occasion honors individual contributions. On a deeper level, celebrations express and reinforce cultural values. What we choose to recognize and reward is witnessed as an expression of the ideals of a company's culture. What is done for one person is elevated for appreciation by the masses. In recognition ceremonies, we experience firsthand what an organization values and cares about.

Drawing a Distinction: Acknowledgment versus Recognition

In our everyday discourse, we intermix the terms *acknowledgment* and *recognition*, obscuring a potentially important distinction between them. As Loretta Malandro says on her audiotape, *The Power in Empowerment*, acknowledgment is an immediate "expression of the profound impact another person has had on you and others." If it is timely, specific, and authentic, on-the-spot acknowledgment motivates and inspires future action: "As I watched you lead the team today, I realized how much you inspire me and others." Or, "You are truly a valuable and gifted person." Or, "I see you running the company some day."

Recognition, on the other hand, consists of "praise and applause for works done in the past, a job well done." It is expressed through speeches, prizes, and other public awards. Malandro believes that there is recognition in most American businesses, but she says that acknowledgment is equally needed and is too often in short supply. Both acknowledgment rituals and recognition ceremonies need to become part of a company's way of life.

Acknowledgment as Company Ritual

Life at Southwest Airlines is chock-full of acknowledgment rituals. Employees compliment each other daily for going the extra mile or doing something special. To Herb Kelleher, Southwest is an everyday celebration of great employees, a daily observance of positive things that happen. Southwest employees acknowledge each other face-to-face all the time. They also do it through handwritten notes and by nominating people to be acknowledged in LUV *Lines*, the company's newsletter. Following are some examples from the book by Kevin and Jackie Freiberg about Southwest.

Eric Brown, Amarillo ramp agent, was acknowledged for going beyond the call of duty to help a stranded customer. Due to fog, the customer's flight was diverted to Amarillo. He had no money, no place to go, and had to be in Lubbock as soon as possible. Eric himself drove the customer to Lubbock and returned to work at five o'clock the next morning.

Debra Undhjem, a Phoenix flight attendant, came to the aid of an eighty-seven-year-old lady who misconnected in Oakland. She eventually made it to Phoenix but missed her flight to Tulsa. Supervision offered to put the customer up at a local hotel at Southwest's expense, but Debra had a better idea; she offered her home. Debra called the woman's family to let them know what was going on and brought her back to the airport the next day. She waited to make sure the customer boarded her flight to Tulsa without a problem. One of Debra's colleagues acknowledged her for going out of her way to help an eighty-seven-year-old diabetic woman spend a comfortable evening in a warm, caring home environment.

At American Airlines, customers join in acknowledgment rites through the company's "You're Someone Special" program. Frequent Flyers are given coupons at regular intervals that they can present to anyone who exemplifies the airline's theme, "Something Special in the Air." On a recent delayed flight from Chicago to Nashville, the flight attendant in the first-class cabin made a special effort to get passengers drinks before takeoff. Her subsequent inflight service was excellent. At the flight's end, four passengers independently presented her with a "Someone Special" coupon. When asked what a coupon was worth, she replied, "Free trips. But that's not the real thing. It's the acknowledgment that counts."

Acknowledgment doesn't have to be fancy or formal. In 1001 *Ways to Reward Employees*, Bob Nelson recounts the story of Elsie Tamayo, the new director of training for the San Diego Department of Social Services who arrived to find a training staff both demoralized and unproductive. She began a series of low-cost interventions geared to rebuilding the staff's identity and self-worth. Within months, the morale, pride, and energy of the training staff soared. Very soon, trainers were held in high regard by the rest of the department.

Tamayo turned the situation around by designating one-half day a month as Reward and Recognition (R&R) Day. The staff could determine the agenda, for example, visiting the zoo or shopping in Tijuana. Each staff meeting started with Tamayo reading letters of praise from clients. She posted handwritten notes on peoples' doors, "You really handled the meeting well," with an explanation of why she thought so. She encouraged the staff to come up with all kinds of ways to acknowledge others. They responded with creative rituals: a parade through-out the building to announce one employee's promotion and a gift of an energizer bunny to another because he kept on "going and going." A roadrunner toy was given to a staff member whose fast work helped keep things moving along (Nelson 1994b, 11–13.)

Sensitive managers seize whatever is at hand to acknowledge a job well done. Some years ago, an engineer at the Foxborough Corporation in Massachusetts entered the chief executive's office bearing exciting news: "I've figured it out. It's the creative breakthrough we've all been waiting for. This new product will position us for years ahead." Sharing the engineer's enthusiasm, the executive smiled and then started fumbling through his desk drawer. "Here," he said. "Congratulations. We're proud of you." He handed the engineer a banana. Stunned, the engineer left the office and walked through the hallway clutching the brown-speckled yellow fruit. Everyone asked where he got it. Still perplexed, he explained the details. People scratched their heads wondering how an over-ripe banana could ever provide just compensation for such a heroic feat. Later that small gesture of acknowledgment was formalized in the company's highest honor: The Gold Banana Award, given for invention and innovation.

Pacific Bell created a "Gotcha!" award, which can be presented by anyone to anyone else in the company "caught" doing a great job. Found deserving, an employee gets a five-dollar certificate from a coworker, who yells "Gotcha!"

In thousands of simple ways, people can be acknowledged for their contributions to each other, customers, and the company. Some people favor regular, spontaneous feedback over more elaborate recognition events. As one manager remarked, "I don't really go for that big-deal celebration stuff. Around here we give a lot of Attaboys. When someone does something special, the executives stick their heads in a door or walk into a meeting and let us know right on the spot." But to others, more elaborate periodic recognition events offer poignant highpoints.

Recognition Ceremonies

Recognition events are often elaborate annual cultural celebrations. The stories that follow illustrate how four different companies celebrate recognition.

Mary Kay Cosmetics Annual Seminar

Mary Kay Ash has built a thriving business on self-esteem. As an unhappy, tired, and restless grandmother in 1963, she started a business aimed as much at selling women on their innate potential as on selling cosmetics for economic profit. In her vision, women would be paid for their brains on a par with men without sacrificing their femininity. Mary Kay says, "We are a people company. Every person wears an invisible sign, 'Make me feel important' . . . and I do."

The Mary Kay Cosmetics Annual Seminar is an event fashioned after a combination of the Miss America pageant, a Broadway show, and the film *Cinderella*. It is more than a typical awards ceremony. Like other meaningful cultural events, it is a celebration of the values and virtues that have made Mary Kay Cosmetics a highly vibrant and prosperous company. The Annual Seminar puts the company's culture on display—symbols, heroines, and stories. In recognizing individuals, it reinforces what the company stands for and dramatizes core cultural values. This same upbeat spirit infuses local Mary Kay rallies and sales meetings. The beauty consultants learn at the Annual Seminar just how powerful recognition can be in stimulating energy and encouraging future performance.

A visitor to the Annual Seminar gave this gripping eyewitness account of the company's yearly drama.

> It was amazing, a parade of women walking across the stage to
> receive diamond bumblebees, pink Cadillacs, and other
> symbolic awards. What was most interesting was that as each
> person received her award, she waved at her group seated
> somewhere in the sea of five thousand women. They cheered
> and waved back. It was like the recognition was as much for

them as for the person receiving the award. The "you can do it" spirit of the company was what seemed to matter the most. That night they crowned the Salesperson of the Year. The recipient was undergoing chemotherapy for breast cancer. As she accepted the award, she pulled off her wig, exposing her baldness. Straight from the heart she said, "Ladies, if I can do this, so can you." The crowd went wild. The organist for the event played "The Impossible Dream." Not a dry eye anywhere.

The next day an evangelist made a speech reinforcing the company's values of "God First, Family Second, Career Third." His wife was onstage and stood quietly by his side as he gave the speech. A little strange, I thought. When the reverend finished, Mary Kay Ash handed the microphone to the wife. She started to tremble. Then she cleared her throat. "I'm very shy," she said. "But last night when I heard Rena's speech, I set some different goals for myself. If she can do it, I can do it too." The crowd rose in a standing ovation that lasted for several minutes.

Saturn's Totem Award

The Retail Strategies, Training, and Consulting Team (RST & C) of the Saturn Corporation is another group that realizes the value of recognition events linked to core values. In 1995, several team volunteers invented the Totem Award to recognize team members who stand out due to a significant action or accomplishment, which can be either a daily responsibility or something completely out of the ordinary. The award nomination form says "We're looking for the WOW! Factor. Something that really made an impact you feel should not go unnoticed." Nominators are asked to identify how the action or accomplishment fits with the company's strategies or values: commitment to customer, enthusiasm, commitment to excel, teamwork, trust and respect for the individual, and continuous improvement.

The idea of the Totem Award originated in the team's desire to foster group cohesion and encourage storytelling. Each unit of the RST & C Team—finance, training, marketing, and retail outlets—was given a large, white cardboard cube and charged with the task of representing on the box the unit's collective identity and individual personalities. They could use whatever symbols the group chose.

In a subsequent event filled with rituals and chants, each unit unveiled its symbolic cube. These were stacked artfully to form the totem pole, which was then further embellished with apertures and feathers. It now sits in a highly visible place in the team's open-space layout.

In January 1997, the first Totem Awards were announced in a ceremonial gathering replete with ritual, pomp, and circumstance. The team did calisthenics together, sang the Saturn song, and participated in the now-familiar Saturn "I say" chant, done to a Native American rhythm. As the awards were given, a feather with the recipient's name was attached to the totem pole. Each award winner then received a certificate and a miniature totem pole. Following are the first award winners and their accomplishments.

Donna Baker consistently demonstrated a positive "can do" attitude that was refreshing and motivating to those around her. As the person who nominated her recounted

> Every time I've needed help from Donna, either in the form of a report, a letter, or a process improvement, she has responded immediately and accurately. Her personal work standards are exemplary and she willingly, cheerfully goes the extra mile to help when she can. She's a tremendous asset to the team. Specifically, she recently helped complete and then walk through the financial approval process. A financial manager was out sick the following day, which was when I needed to fax the registration and financial voucher information to meet a deadline that would save about $200. When I came in Saturday to do it, guess what? She'd already taken care of it!!

Karin Griffin and Larry Davis demonstrated their dedication to teamwork, a fundamental tenet of Saturn's philosophy: the belief that effective teams engage the talents of individual members while encouraging team growth. A colleague gave testimony to their accomplishment:

> Retail Strategies, Training, and Consulting would like to recognize Karin and Larry for their contributions to designing and constructing the Totem Pole we see before us today. Karin and Larry met the challenge by using their individual talents and their personal time to ensure the totem pole would be

constructed smoothly. Special thanks to Karin for her inspiring vision for the construction of the totem pole. Special thanks to Larry for spending time at home constructing the base structure of the totem pole. His extra efforts made the final build run smoothly.

Jim Cranor, then leader of the RST & C Team, summarized for us the rationale behind the Totem Award ceremony: "There are too many companies that think an expensive weed whacker or trip to Hawaii is what people want as an award. We want our awards to have meaning and reflect our shared values and strategies."

Honeywell's Lund Award

> **Behind every good person there is some other person who shapes their life.**
>
> —*Ed Lund*

Ed Lund is a retired Honeywell executive after whom the company's annual award for developing people is named. Across the company, Lund is known for his commitment to the growth and development of Honeywell employees. He served as a mentor to many of the company's leaders. The Lund Award reinforces the company's values of integrity, mutual respect, open communication, diversity, innovation, continuous improvement, teamwork, and performance.

Each year, business units around the world select people who exemplify the spirit of Ed Lund, that is, people who (1) develop people, serve as role models and coaches, and consistently meet or exceed business and organizational objectives as performance leaders; (2) demonstrate the value and commitment Honeywell places on the growth and development of its employees; and (3) acknowledge the significant role of leadership in the development of Honeywell employees.

Award recipients each receive a cash stipend of three thousand dollars. Even more significant, the winners and a guest of their choice are invited to a week-long celebration at the company's headquarters in Minneapolis, Minnesota. For a week, honorees from around the world are feted with an array of special doings and activities: storytelling, tours, fabulous meals, and outside guest speakers. Top corporate executives give presentations on business happenings and their relationship to core values, inspired leadership, and teamwork. The event culminates in a lavish awards banquet. Pictures of the award winners are displayed in a Hall of Fame area in the company's headquarters. It is just one of the award programs the company sponsors. A visit to the Hall of Fame reveals pictures of people who, in a variety of ways, demonstrate what the company values and rewards.

In 1996, award winners included one Honeywell manager who had to cut his staff by one-half, laying off twenty-five people. "I was the last one who expected to receive a Lund Award," he said. The award was given because of the caring and compassionate manner in which he handled the situation. All those laid off received counseling and supportive help, and were placed in jobs outside the company. The manager received letters of praise from all those who were let go.

Southwest Airlines Deserves the Quadruple Crown Award

Effective recognition events are inclusive; they assure that applause is not limited to those in the limelight. Too often, however, salespeople or frontline employees are the primary recipients of awards. Those who labor behind the scenes are left out—unrewarded and unrecognized for their important accomplishments. (See *Managing the Hidden Organization: Strategies for Empowering Your Behind-the-Scenes Employees* by Terrence Deal and William Jenkins.)

Southwest Airlines is a five-time winner of the airline industry's Triple Crown Prize: bags delivered to the right place, on-time departures and arrivals, and customer satisfaction. But Southwest Airlines deserves a fourth crown for its stellar efforts to celebrate across-the-board employee accomplishments.

One of the company's most festive celebrations is the Annual Awards Banquet. Service pins are awarded to employees who have been with the company for ten, twenty, or twenty-five years. But longevity is not the only virtue the event spotlights. The Founders Award, the most coveted, is bestowed on employees who consistently go beyond the call of duty. The Presidents Award is conferred on those who demonstrate Southwest's virtues and values: compassion, support, and a terrific sense of humor and passion for fun.

In addition to the formal awards banquet, Southwest sponsors other occasions for recognizing special achievements. A Leadership Award is presented to people whose efforts go well beyond the ambitious reach of the company's mission statement. A Community Relations Extraordinaire Award has been granted to someone whose community involvement work is exemplary. Good Neighbor

Awards, Sense of Humor Awards, Hairdresser of the Year Awards, and Positively Outrageous Service Awards extend the recognition to all areas of the company.

Those who work backstage—outside the public's eye—have a special event to fete their accomplishments. Each year, a Heroes of the Heart Celebration recognizes a backstage operation for its contributions to Southwest's success. One year, station administrators received the award. A brand new Boeing 737 was named for them and flew in their honor for a year. A Top Wrench Award is presented to top mechanics. A Top Cleaner Award is conferred on cleaners who keep the company's planes immaculate. There is plenty of recognition to go around at Southwest, with celebrations that include everyone. And it is all done with a special touch: balloons, fun, festival, and spirit. As one employee observed, "This company is a daily celebration of great employees" (Freiberg and Freiberg 1996, 192).

Team-Based Recognition

With the advent of the quality movement and self-directed work teams, top leaders are challenged to broaden the base of recognition. Attention often needs to shift to groups—showcasing valued contributions of teams or even the entire organization. One way to do this is to encourage employee-to-employee recognition within teams: Other team members select deserving recipients and often confer the award themselves.

An employee at Parkview Episcopal Hospital in Pueblo, Colorado, explains what the hospital does to recognize teams.

> We never had money, but the first and third Wednesdays of every month the administration gave our teams a chance to start up, report progress, or finish their improvement/redesign projects—way-to-go milestones. The whole hospital came for the two-way education and communication. Teams did skits and humorous or straight presentations—their choice. We celebrated teams completing their work with the gift of their choice (pizza for all, gift certificates, movie passes) and words of thanks from the CEO. Pictures with the CEO and team were published in the weekly newsletter.

Once a year we had Quality Week, with a parade to start, where each of sixty business units got five minutes to highlight their quality efforts. We had food, fun, laughter, and merriment for all shifts.

Other companies have encouraged similar practices, with notes of thanks or praise taking various forms. Following are several examples, condensed from Matt Weinstein's book *Managing to Have Fun*:

IBM's Storage Systems division in San Jose, California, created a frequent flyer program. On Fridays, a model airplane trophy was awarded to an employee who deserved thanks. The award was conferred by the prior Friday's recipient, complete with a brief description (flight plan) of what the current recipient had done to deserve the trophy. Miles were awarded to both the giver and the receiver, and double miles were conferred for presenting the award to someone outside the giver's department. The miles could then be exchanged for gifts. The "high flyers" were posted each week on the company bulletin board. After a year, employees found ample reason to appreciate each other, and even without the trophy began to spontaneously acknowledge each other.

A company known for its noncompetitive human interaction games, Matt Weinstein's Playfair creates community and shared history through the use of rituals, one of which is a summer staff retreat. The first day of the retreat is filled with traditions: an opening ceremony where everyone in the company receives a flood of positive feedback; a welcoming ceremony for new employees; ceremonies for important service anniversaries (such as ten years with the company); and the presentation of a commemorative gift to all in attendance. Tremendous thought is given to the symbolism of the gift. For example, one year the slogan was "The future's so bright, we're gonna' need shades," and the gift was sunglasses imprinted with the company logo.

Another ritual, described by Matt Weinstein as the most moving event ever, entailed presentation of the Playfair jackets. As each staff member received their jacket, they draped it on their shoulders like a cape and went to the center of a big circle, while the other staff called out with support, appreciation, and positive feedback. The person in the center pulled out another jacket, read the embroidered name of the owner, and the same process unfolded. While it took most of the afternoon, "It was a wonderful afternoon, filled with laughter, tears, and open-hearted appreciation" (p. 165).

Sharing the limelight is another way to elevate the work of teams. Quality Days are opportunities for teams to celebrate collective efforts at improving processes and delighting customers. As noted, applause, called "walking music," accompanies a trip across the stage to collect an award at Mary Kay Cosmetics Annual Seminars, and this award is shared with the winner's home team. Team pictures in a new product ad or in the company newsletter, or team recognition in front of visiting dignitaries or on a team-building retreat are additional ways that teams can bathe in the limelight and share a feeling of importance in the community.

Regular Acknowledgment and Recognition Pay Off

People crave social reinforcement, affirmation that they are important, that their efforts really matter. Made public, such expressions can have a tremendous impact. There is no limit to the number of ways one can reward, recognize, and value a workforce, as shown in Bob Nelson's book, 1001 *Ways to Reward Employees*. The point is to do it regularly.

With the amount of money wasted annually adopting the latest fad, hiring the most expensive consulting firm, or giving executives exorbitant bonuses, any company should be able to find the resources to support acknowledgment rituals and recognition ceremonies. If they are attuned to core values and done with style, the return on investment is spectacular.

Recognition and acknowledgment show people the company cares. As Lee Bolman and Terrence Deal advocate in *Leading with Soul*:

If you show people you don't care, they'll return the favor.
Show them you care about them, they'll reciprocate.

Chapter 5

High Points: Celebrating Triumphs and Successes

When we think of ritual and ceremony, our thoughts usually turn to new beginnings: birth, marriage, launching a new product, founding a company. Or we think about celebrating success: winning a championship, besting yearly financial goals, beating the competition. This is a well-known, upbeat side of ritual and ceremony—toasting our triumphs, accentuating our collective accomplishments.

Convening special occasions around moments of success serves a vital role in organizations. It draws

> There is a tide in the affairs of men, which, taken at its flood, leads on to fortune.
>
> —William Shakespeare

people together, reminds them of why the company is in business, allows them to witness their individual contribution to the big picture, builds team spirit, and renews faith and hope. Our most cherished memories are often forged in celebrations of high-water marks.

Celebration at Saturn

Many successful companies today recognize the benefits of celebrating new starts, successful launches, and important wins. The Saturn Corporation, General Motor's showplace of progressive people policies and high-quality standards, has caught America's attention. Staffed with union members from the "Old World" of GM, Saturn is building cars that compete, in terms of customer satisfaction and quality standards, with higher sticker-price cars such as Infinity and Lexus. A great deal of Saturn's success can be attributed to the company's high-touch people policies, flat structure, legendary teamwork, and cooperative politics—especially the close working relationship between management and the UAW. But equal credit goes to more intangible aspects of Saturn's culture, what some employees call the car manufacturer's soul.

From the very beginning, Saturn has relied on celebrations to acknowledge significant milestones in its development. As the first crimson four-door Saturn rolled off the assembly line, festivities captured the hearts of all those whose hard work had made the moment possible. The rollout ceremony created lingering memories that sustain employees' spirits to this day. Jack O'Toole, in his book *Forming the Future,* describes the magic of the launch:

> I will never forget that day as long as I live. . . . I was totally caught up in the pride and confidence that literally oozed from [everyone]. The applause and whistles and laughter and tears at Inspiration Point and down the aisles leading to the audit area were deafening. But I don't think anyone was prepared for the decibel level that was experienced when that car slowly wheeled into audit [the final quality checkpoint], with Roger [Smith] and Owen [Bieber] smiling and waving, followed by every team member in the plant who had previously lined the aisles. When Roger stepped out of that car, raised both of his fists jubilantly into the air and shouted "We did it!" the house came down. All were on their feet cheering and laughing, and as I looked around, with tears streaming down my face

> unashamedly, there wasn't a dry eye in the house. Everyone
> was crying, hugging, laughing, crying again, hugging someone
> else; and the sound was absolutely deafening. As Roger and
> Owen ascended the stage, where they were greeted by
> [management and union officials], the standing ovation
> continued and grew louder. Then Roger turned to all the team
> members and the press, pumped his fist repeatedly in the air,
> blew everyone a great big kiss, and mouthed an unheard "Thank
> you." The noise grew louder yet (p. 43).

Keep in mind that GM's CEO, Roger Smith, described in this gripping account, is the same widely criticized, rational, aloof, out-of-touch, financially oriented executive who once championed robots over people. He was the center of attention in the sarcastic feature movie *Roger and Me*. Yet as the first Saturn rolled off the line, the typically stoic Roger Smith became, according to O'Toole, "a poor child who one day awoke in the middle of Macy's toy department with a blank check" (p. 144).

At the launch event, Roger was hugged and kissed, his renowned red complexion turning even more crimson than usual. As reported by Lee Bolman and Terrence Deal in *Reframing Organizations*, one Saturn employee remarked, "I hated Roger Smith, but that day I cheered my lungs out for him" (p. 4). The day's event even touched people who watched the ceremony off-site at General Motors. The following remarks by a Saturn employee are reported in *Managing the Hidden Organization* by Deal and Jenkins:

> I remember someone telling later that up in Detroit, they had
> shown it live on TV, and those Detroit people saw us down here
> crying, and they were skeptical about the sincerity, until they
> looked around the room and saw those Saturn people who were
> in Detroit and saw tears coming down from them as well. It was
> a very emotional day. We had worked so hard, and to actually
> see the final product was just overwhelming. What was even
> more special was that team members from various areas in the
> factory were the ones that pulled tarps off the new cars, not top
> management (p. 238).

One of Saturn's internally recognized challenges is how to keep the spirit of the first car's rollout alive—particularly with new hires who missed out on those initial festivities. The company is obviously trying to respond to the challenge. More recent ceremonies provide vivid evidence that it is having some success. Take, for example, the widely heralded Saturn Homecoming. In 1994, Saturn owners were invited to visit the Spring Hill plant to see where their car was born. Over forty thousand people from all over the country responded. They drove their Saturns to one of the largest and most unique corporate celebrations on record. Food, music, plant tours, games, and other activities drew employees and customers together in a family gathering. Even an intense thundershower that flattened tents, drenched everyone, created a giant mud hole, and resulted in many injuries could not dampen the spirit of the event. Jack O'Toole recounts the following story:

> [Homecoming] really hit the spot and gave everyone a real
> boost, just before the model changeover the first two weeks of
> July. Without this emotional release, many of our hard-working
> folks would have left for shutdown and replayed the turmoil of
> the last six months over and over in their heads and would have
> come back unrested, weary, and more confused than ever. What
> a weekend it was! The entertainment was great, as was the food,
> our retailers, every public official and politician within five
> states, but the real purpose of these 44,000 owners and their
> families was to meet the men and women who had built the cars
> they liked so much. They stood in lines for up to four hours in
> 90-degree heat and 80 percent humidity just to walk through the
> plants, take pictures of the technicians, talk with them, and sign
> every inch of white space in every facility, in memory and thanks
> (O'Toole 1996, 194).

The celebration of the company's one millionth car was also accorded comparable pomp and circumstance. But as life at Saturn becomes more routine and memories of Homecoming, The First Car, or The Millionth Car begin to fade, will the company continue its commitment to celebrating its successes? It is a question that managers ask frequently and is one of the reasons behind Saturn's biannual bridge-building event, where new employees particularly can experience directly the spirit that propels the company to new heights. Old-timers and newcomers work together to build a bridge between the past and the future. As the bridge is constructed, stories flow. When the bridge is complete, everyone walks across the structure, commemorating the journey from old roots to new vistas.

Saturn's corporate design evolved from an extensive investigation of best practices around the world. As a group of ninety-nine employees and managers combed the world's best businesses, they learned that celebration is one of the most powerful ways to renew the collective spirit. It is a common-sense lesson that other companies can learn from Saturn's success.

Boeing's Official Rollout: The 777

Other manufacturing companies have also learned the lessons of celebration. In manufacturing, the time span between design and final product can be lengthy, and during this period conflicts can erupt between different units, nerves can fray, energy can lag, and momentum can wane. To complete a top-quality product on time, aircraft-manufacturing businesses such as Boeing build in frequent opportunities to stop work, take stock of progress, and celebrate that progress. The design and production of the 777 airliner was a state-of-the-art operation from start to finish, due both to its technological innovation and Boeing's progressive human resource practices.

At various milestones during the months-long production process, managers and workers took time to celebrate progress, build morale, and refocus energy for the tasks ahead. Sometimes these were brief work breaks with sandwiches and drinks. At other times, the ceremonies were more elaborate with stories, speeches, music, and more lengthy conviviality.

The official rollout of the 777 was an elaborate affair, a dramatic testimony to the thousands of individual and group efforts that gave the plane flight. No one at Boeing will ever forget the day's events. Lore surrounding the first rollout in 1994 will live forever to embellish and reinforce the company's long-standing tradition. In *Twenty-First Century Jet*, Karl Sabbagh quotes a manager who says, "The launch was special. Unlike the other milestones, it was an event whose symbolism was far more important than any specific achievements in the construction of the plane" (p. 25).

The actual unveiling of the plane was preceded by preliminary events. Thirty-five hundred people in a lavishly decorated hangar watched videos depicting various stages of the production process. The rest is described here by Sabbagh:

> At twenty past six [A.M.] the music changed and moving images started to appear on the screens: a combination of black and white videos—a clever move to avoid pre-empting the all-color vision of the plane itself—and color slides with one-word attributes of the plane and its manufacture, such as "Teamwork" and "Trust" (although for a moment, because of the darker "T," this almost looked like "rust"). Frank Sinatra sang "Come Fly With Me," a narrator spoke about the 777, interspersed with comments of workers and managers, and time-lapse cinematography of the assembly of the plane was run. The music got louder and grander and black drapes behind the white ones rose, revealing a dim image of the 777. It could have been another projection, since it was only dimly lit, with a crisscross pattern. Then the white drape lifted and the plane was there, still not quite real, bathed in colored lights. The whole area erupted into gasps and rapturous applause, with whoops of excitement. Many people wept. Lights went on in each of the interior areas in turn, starting with the cockpit, where a central-casting pilot and co-pilot were seen to be waving like Disney animatronic hominoids. The music reached a climax as the plane was bathed in very bright light and the narrator instructed the people to "Come on up" (pp. 258–59).

People surged forward to view the result of their long and hard labor. As with the other celebrations of triumph we have described, the event covered the basics: food, music, drama, universal attendance, intense emotions, and special effects. After everyone had their moment with the plane, it was towed off and filled with fuel for the first time. A festive rollout. The next big party would witness the plane's first official flight.

Celebrating New Aircraft and Routes at Southwest

All companies do not produce dramatic new products such as a Boeing 777. But all businesses have their special moments of growth, progress, and glory. The arrival of new aircraft at Southwest is more than a matter of expanding passenger capacity. New planes are another convenient cause for well-planned ceremonies attuned to both the company's history and other magic moments in the history of flight.

As Southwest continues to expand its service, new routes receive the same kind of ceremonial attention as do new planes. When Southwest's Nashville operation launched service to Orlando, Florida, the city's air terminal was the site of an appropriate send-off: The Beach Blast. The company's personnel were dressed in beachwear, wore straw hats and sunglasses, and painted zinc oxide sunscreen on their noses. Food was abundant and in line with Florida's unique culinary style. Numbered boarding passes were ripe oranges rather than the regular plastic cards. Calypso music created the mood for a limbo contest. The winner was an elderly lady confined to a wheelchair who was pushed under the bar by a Southwest employee. She received both a prize and an ovation.

Rather than customers and employees, the crowd resembled a bunch of youthful beachgoers caught up in a party mood. One passenger got so caught up in the event's culminating congo line dance that he forgot to board the flight, the last one to Orlando. "Oh, what the hell," he said. "I'll catch the flight tomorrow. Missing a day at the office is no big deal. Missing a moment of this kind of stuff would be a sin." He trotted off to spend the night at a hotel near the airport. He refused Southwest's offer to pay for the room.

> I believe that the ultimate in self-actualization is when a person is confused about the difference between employment and recreation.
>
> —Ken Blanchard

Wal-Mart's Festivities

At Wal-Mart, the late Sam Walton became a legend for making weekly store visits and leading employees in the Wal-Mart cheer. The ceremonial commitment was reflected up and down the corporate hierarchy. Each Thursday, vice presidents would visit stores and then return to Bentonville, Arkansas, for weekly Saturday morning executive meetings that included senior executives, the merchandising staff, headquarters staff, and Walton. In *Wal-Mart*, Sandra Vance and Roy Scott talk about the company's rituals and ceremonies.

> An informal tone would be struck at the onset by Walton, who would lead the assembled in the traditional "Wal-Mart cheer": "Give me a W!" Walton would shout. "W!" the group would shout back. "Give me an A!"—and so forth until the company's name had been spelled out (p. 68).

While almost corny and contrived on the surface, employees inside the company looked forward to Walton's visits. The same celebratory spirit was evident in Wal-Mart's annual shareholder meetings.

> By the late 1980s [annual meetings] had taken on the trappings of a religious revival for Wal-Mart's ardent supporters. These robust gatherings had grown to such proportions that the 1989 affair attracted more than 7,000 people. At this meeting, the proceedings began solemnly enough with the Pledge of Allegiance and a prayer. Then, for two hours, exuberant shareholders were treated to a rollicking program of songs, awards, and, of course, price comparisons indicating that Wal-Mart's prices were lower than its competitors' on selected merchandise (pp. 106–7).

At one annual event, Walton himself got caught up in the enthusiasm. He promised to dance on Wall Street in a hula skirt if Wal-Mart achieved an 8 percent pretax profit. That year, profit turned out to be slightly above that—8.04 percent. "Walton resolutely kept his word. In March 1984, he donned a Hawaiian shirt and a grass skirt over his business suit and, looking every bit as uncomfortable as he no doubt felt, briefly danced on Wall Street" (p. 207). Walton's spirit is evident in Wal-Mart operations to this day: Rituals launch a new business day in Wal-Mart stores and the weekend meetings continue as a source of energy and pride.

Technology Can Undercut Celebration

In our modern business world, which is too often dominated by meaningless techniques and a pervasive concern for the quarterly bottom line, it is easy to put ritual and ceremony on the corporate back burner. Technology, with all its virtues and blessings, can undercut gatherings for special events. The story of what happened at the Naval Weapons Center at China Lake, California, is a good example.

China Lake built its stellar reputation on the development of the Sidewinder missile. The weapon was invented and assembled by one of the center's teams on a shoestring budget without official authorization. Its success was a momentous triumph and a source of pride for both military and civilian personnel who worked at the center. Memories of the celebrations lingered for a long time.

But several years ago, a group of China Lake's leaders began to sense that something was missing. After some soul-searching, they identified a potential cause. In the old days, the testing of a weapons system was a centerwide occasion. The operation closed down as employees gathered to witness the launch. Dignitaries attended. There was food, drink, and music. A successful launch was greeted with cheers. Spirits soared. People congratulated each other and returned to work with renewed energy and gusto: "That was fun, let's rev up, work hard, and do it again soon."

During more recent times, computer simulations replaced the old-fashioned launch event. Technology appeared to serve the same function at a greatly reduced cost. On a rational basis, it did. But as the center's leadership reflected for a while, they began to wonder about some hidden costs of the new ways. Had technical progress deprived people of a collective opportunity to celebrate, without a suitable substitute? This realization launched a renewed commitment to celebrate attainments and accentuate the center's unique identity.

Toasting Triumphs: A Final Word

Across these examples, there is a consistent theme: Triumphs, successes, and new beginnings demand some form of collective recognition. Gathering people together to celebrate releases emotions, summons the corporate spirit, and creates stories and memories that kindle faith, hope, zeal, and enthusiasm for future efforts and performance. Many celebrations come at the high point, the zenith of performance. At such times, nothing is held back as people revel in the glory. Other celebrations happen as new things emerge—the unveiling of a new service, strategy, or vision. Again, it is a time to relish progress and to renew the faith that success is within reach.

Chapter 6

Coping with Calamity and Loss: Rituals of Comfort and Letting Go

elebration of victory and success comes fairly easy. But what happens when things are on the wane? Nothing ever works perfectly. Strategies some-

> **Above the cloud with its shadow is the star with its light.**
>
> —Victor Hugo

times fail to accomplish intended goals; products can be unable to capture market share. Even worse, costly errors or disasters can occur or needed reforms can flag in the face of opposition. Such corporate calamities don't often receive our conscious attention or recognition. Misfortunes are rarely officially acknowledged as part of our everyday work world. Shriveling things are shunted to the side, left to wither away without bothering anyone. Mistakes are covered up or explained away. Yet everyone knows such glitches exist; there are skeletons in every corporate closet.

Our failure to acknowledge demise and disaster in the same way we recognize new initiatives and triumphs silently takes its toll.

Even further outside our conscious awareness are programs or practices that have died on the vine. Every organization has its share of new starts that didn't pan out or old traditions that fell by the wayside having outlived their usefulness, left behind in a parade of innovation and technical progress. These often decay unburied in the corporate graveyard, universally known but rarely acknowledged. Without any collective ritual to help them grieve, let go, heal, and move on, people often feel a deep sense of loss. Figure 3 depicts the enduring cycle of corporate booms and busts.

Historically, human beings have convened ritual and ceremony at life's darkest, as well as its brightest, moments. For individuals facing terminal illness, hospice associations provide rituals of comfort and support. As we lose loved ones or cherished possessions, society dictates transition rites: wakes, funerals, mourning periods, and acts of commemoration and remembrance. Think about the poignant gathering following the bombing of the Federal Building in Oklahoma City. Families of victims joined hands with the president of the United States and the first lady. An a cappella rendition of the national anthem helped people's spirits soar to distant vistas. At the ceremony's conclusion, everyone melded his or her voice as the crowd sang "Amazing Grace." Tears and sorrow intermingled with solidarity, comfort, and hope. A year after the bombing, a ceremony at the site acknowledged the anniversary of that tragic event.

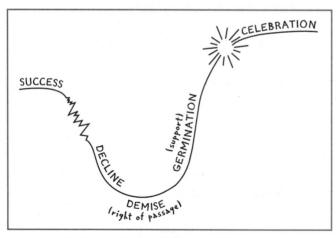

Figure 3. Cyclical Ups and Downs in Corporate Life

Yet disaster, demise, and death receive little official recognition in the work-place. Ritual and ceremony are typically reserved for moments of victory or joyous occasions. At such events, the human spirit soars to accentuate a positive moment. But spirit is also a comforting and healing balm. Especially in a world of rapid change, we need to pay as much attention to loss as to gain, to demise as to growth, to disaster as to triumph. Otherwise, people are deprived of the cere-monial support of letting go, reaching closure, maintaining hope, and moving on.

Recognizing the Pits

Southwest Airlines celebrates disasters as well as victories. The company experi-enced unusual chaos following an announcement in July 1996 of twenty-five dollar fares—anywhere. Janna Lewis, Nashville's marketing director, described the unanticipated aftermath.

> Friday morning we broke the fare sale to the press. Friday
> afternoon we were jammed, people lined up out the door at the
> airport. We got sixty-six thousand calls in an hour. Shut down
> Sabre. Shut down AT&T. The FCC started raising questions.
> I have the capacity for thirty voice mail messages in my office.
> I had to hire a temporary all week to take messages out of my
> voice mail. She did nothing else. By Wednesday she was crying
> because we were being cussed, screamed at, stomped on,
> jumped on.

Later that week, Herb Kelleher issued a formal apology to the airline's reg-ular customers. Bosses issued survival kits containing gum, granola bars, pop-corn, and other fast foods to employees, who were working well beyond normal hours to answer calls and deal with customers. The survival kits served as humor-ous ritual, buoying people's spirits and creating additional energy to weather the temporary storm.

Southwest's unsurpassed ability to turn potential calamity into a vibrant, festive occasion is exemplified in its "Malice in Dallas" arm-wrestling contest. For many years, Stevens Aviation, a company that services private aircraft in the Southeast, has championed the slogan "We're just plane smart." Imagine their surprise when they saw an advertisement for Southwest on television claiming, "We're just plane smart." The traditional scenario is obvious: litigation. But instead Kurt Herwald, CEO of Stevens, challenged Southwest's Kelleher to an arm-wrestling contest to settle the dispute. They rented an arena in Dallas, bused in employees, and arm wrestled for the right to use the catchy slogan. Herwald won, but then announced that Southwest could continue to use the slogan. They settled the dispute, donated $15,000 to charity, received millions of dollars worth of free publicity, and reinforced the unique spirit of both companies.

A similar response to calamity is echoed in Eastman Kodak's handling of the Black and White Division's turnaround. At a company gathering in August 1989, Colby Chandler, then Eastman Kodak's mild-mannered CEO, communicated his displeasure with the entire company's dismal performance when he hacked the podium to pieces. The message: We're in deep trouble and need a fundamental shift in direction. Black and White took up the challenge, chose the zebra as its new symbol, and transformed the division.

Two years later, previous performance standards had been surpassed, and the division was being heralded as one of Kodak's shining stars as well as one of the company's best places to work. Those in charge of the "Team Zebra" transformation sensed early on that change brings loss as well as gain. Celebrations provided an opportunity for people to mourn the old ways and build the spirit needed to maintain forward momentum. At one of the group's frequent celebrations, fun and frivolity were capped off with a more serious closing event, described by Stephen Frangos in his account, *Team Zebra*, "We donned sweatshirts bearing our new logo and took a team picture. We then held a mock funeral for the ways of the past" (p. 17).

There are important lessons to be learned from these examples: Rituals of comfort and consolation draw people together during dark moments, providing hope and faith for better times ahead, just as festivals do at apexes of triumph. Ritual and ceremony also generate healing power in times of change. In life and at work, people become attached to familiar faces, patterns, and ways. Change ruptures symbolic attachments and locks us into one of two reactions: Either hold on and keep things as much the same as possible or plunge busily into the new reality, severing historical roots. These twin impulses can cause people to either get stuck in the past or find themselves floating aimlessly in an anchorless present.

For companies, this creates a difficult dilemma. To compete and thrive, we have to transform. But if we change too much, we run the risk of wounding our people and losing our competitive edge. These significant human costs are evident in the alteration of established products (the new Coke), the revision of corporate identities (the merger of Northwest and Republic Airlines), and the loss of cherished symbols (Bob's Big Boy or Ma Bell). In all cases, the absence of widely held public transition rites took an enormous human toll. People rebelled against the new Coke and the company lost market share for a time. At Northwest, employees got even through sabotage: sending bags in the wrong direction, purposely giving mediocre service. Customers of Bob's Big Boy restaurants boycotted until the Chubby Checker symbol was restored. Within AT&T, the costs of divestiture were even more dramatic.

Divestiture at AT&T

The 1982 breakup of the Bell System was an event unparalleled in American business history. In response to a decision by Judge Green, a one-hundred-year-old institution was broken apart; local operating companies were separated from their AT&T parent. The change also severed ties between Bell employees and cherished cultural ways and symbols that heretofore had elicited tremendous collective loyalty, commitment, and pride: a shared sense of history and tradition; universal service as the company's core value; heroes, such as installer Angus McDonald, whose legendary snowshoe trek through the New York "Blizzard of '88" was universally heralded and became a widely shared exemplar of assuring telephone service irrespective of weather conditions or other threats; shared rituals, such as meetings about safety with a symbolic subtext of bonding and acculturation, or an operations conference serving as an annual companywide celebration. Then there were stories such as the "Miracle on Second Avenue," a legendary tale extolling the commitment of Bell employees from all over the country who rallied to restore telephone service after a devastating fire in one of New York's switching complexes. And, of course, there was the company's widely recognized symbol of continuity, compassion, and dedication—Ma Bell.

The message that "Ma Bell doesn't live here anymore" was devastating to employees. In divestiture's wake came suicides, divorces, and alcohol abuse—symptoms of people grieving for a cherished lost past. In response to an open-ended item on a post-divestiture questionnaire distributed to employees across the system, people poured out their anguish, as reported by W. Brooke Tunstall in *Disconnecting Parties*.

"My heart's broken."

"I feel like I'm being torn apart."

"I [feel] like I [have] gone through a divorce that neither my wife nor children [want]."

"It was forced on us by some very powerful outside force and I could not control the outcome."

"It [is] like waking up in familiar surroundings (your home) but your family and all you held dearly [are] missing" (pp. 153–154).

In response to the personal and collective anguish, Bell subunits struggled to find a source of healing. One division held a full-scale Mardi Gras celebration ending in a New Orleans funeral procession, complete with jazz band and a coffin figuratively containing Ma Bell's remains. Another division produced a video entitled *Farewell Ma Bell*. It featured employees lip-synching "good-bye" songs. It became one of the most powerful, widely applicable examples of how simultaneously to stir up unconscious feelings of loss and stimulate the process of healing. Informally, many people at AT&T found ways to mourn their loss and move on. Unfortunately, AT&T's leaders too often missed opportunities to convene systemwide occasions for coping with cultural loss. Theirs was not an uncommon omission.

Many managers and business executives overlook the symbolic aftermath lurking in the wake of change. Some time ago, for example, IBM divested itself of a small company in its portfolio. Upper managers tried to assure employees that new ownership would not represent significant change. Employees felt differently. One remarked

Imagine being a small boy taken for a walk by your father. He takes you to a strange house and says, "This is where you will live from now on. Don't worry. It's an equivalent house, and he's an equally good father. Goodbye." (Deal and Jenkins 1994, 2).

Culturally aware companies view demise and loss as an opportunity to convene rituals and ceremonies of transition—to help people let go, heal, and connect with a new reality.

School Closings in Fulton County

Fulton County Public Schools in Atlanta, Georgia, demonstrate how even unprecedented loss can be handled in a symbolically sensitive way. Closing a school is difficult for any community. Schools are repositories of memories, museums of virtue, symbols of community pride. Closing even one school can tear a community apart and jeopardize a superintendent's career. But Fulton County had no other choice. Because of severe enrollment declines, a result of expansion at the Atlanta airport that eliminated many of the family homes in the area, Fulton County was forced to close thirty-four schools in one year—including the district's oldest high school.

Criteria were established to determine which schools would be closed. People agreed on the criteria, until they learned their own school was to be sacrificed. In the midst of the process, following the official announcement, community uproar reached a crescendo. Rage was muted somewhat with an announcement by the district's superintendent, Dr. Jim Fox, that the school board had voted to create a museum within each local community losing its school to house a permanent collection of cherished artifacts.

As each school was closed, the district sponsored a fitting final ceremony. In one school, parents, students, city dignitaries, and alumni formed a parade and marched together onto the school grounds. Music, speeches, and stories from graduates peppered a poignant program. As the event drew to a close, the school's custodial staff wrapped the entire red brick building in a large red ribbon. The assembly joined hands and sang "Auld Lang Syne." The next day, the school was torn down. Later, each person who attended the ceremony received a photograph of the school wrapped in its red ribbon . . . along with a single brick from the building wrapped in the same way.

In our modern world, we experience change at an unprecedented pace. Too often, we fail to recognize the enormous toll it exacts. Like those in Fulton County, we rarely have much choice—we must change. But we do have options for how we manage the process. Change leaves existential wounds that only the symbolic power of ritual and ceremony can heal. Even welcome changes require meaningful transition events to help people let go of old ways.

Letting Go of Old Baggage

Every human group creates a culture to give meaning and purpose to life in general as well as to life at work. This social tapestry, woven from day-to-day happenings and relationships, provides cohesion and focus, paving the way for a healthy, vibrant workplace. Under some conditions, however, cultural practices and ways can cast a negative pall over an enterprise, creating a sick situation. People create meaning one way or another. Devils can hold people together as tightly as heroes or heroines. Bitching and moaning can become the daily ritual if there is not a more positive, upbeat substitute.

In one U.S. company, chaos reigned following the departure of the corporate "Satan." Before this unofficial devil's retirement (Harry was his name, and he was the vice president for finance), his supervisor, the CEO, was credited for everything that went well. Harry, meanwhile, received the blame for everything that went awry. He took the fall when the company's logo was affixed upside down on the entire fleet of corporate automobiles and trucks. The installation of urinals in the women's rest rooms of the new office complex was seen as Harry's doing. The mysterious downturn of sales in the midst of an economic boom was laid at his feet, as was the failure of Research and Development to produce a new product before the competition. Once Harry retired, there was no one to blame for errors and screwups. Conflict intensified. Fingers of blame pointed from one victim to the next. Finally, Harry was invited back (with a good bit of prompting), given a party, and roasted in a hilarious celebration. People get attached to negative symbols as well as positive cultural icons. The event served as an exorcism, paving the way for the emergence of a more positively oriented workplace.

Change is loss, and even the transition from vice to virtue has to be publicly acknowledged in ritual and ceremony. There is an age-old universal script for ceremonies that address giving up or ridding an organization of something undesirable. Cultural variations include burying, burning, trashing, or otherwise destroying and thereby dealing with unwanted symbols, practices, or ways.

Mac Pirkle, director of Tennessee's Repertory Theater, described to us a ceremony he convened for his actors on a retreat.

> We took our cue from the Cherokee Green Corn Ceremony, held
> at the beginning of each year. Participants brought in a
> symbolic representation of something they wanted to get rid
> of—baggage, as we called it. The Cherokees also brought

something that represented how they wanted to be nourished and something to give to someone else. We loaded our "baggage" on a sled and dragged it to a campfire, where each person took their symbolic element off the sled and threw it into the fire. We invented a phrase of affirmation, "I'm here to get rid of whatever." And the others would shout "Yes" in reply, until we were rid of the undesirables.

Phil Condit, Boeing's new CEO, is widely heralded as a "people person" who believes that positive relationships and hands-on leadership will help the company prosper in an intensely competitive industry. To prosper, Boeing must build planes rapidly while radically transforming the way they are built. We have seen already how Boeing celebrated its way to one successful product—the 777. Condit also understands how to help people let go of old baggage. A September 30, 1996, article in *Business Week* says the following:

> During a series of week-long meetings in 1994 and 1995, senior managers capped their sessions with a trip to Condit's house for dinner, then gathered outside around a giant fire pit to tell stories about Boeing. [Condit and David Whyte] asked them to write negative stories and toss them into the flames to banish the "dark" side of Boeing's past (p. 122).

Coping with Change

Shutdowns

A health care executive described the last gathering of her business unit:

> We gathered at my house to bury our business as we knew it. We did not make budget and the company decision was to disassemble our group. We were not sure where each of us would go, whether we would have continued employment, what would happen to our clients. But we knew there would be no more "us" as a functional unit. After dinner with our families, just the staff gathered on the carpet of the study to say a few parting words. It is our nature to love community. We talked about all we had created together—some beautiful, innovative

products for our customers. How now we had the opportunity to take what we have out into the world. And who knows, we might end up together again—after all, 3M started out as a mining business that turned into sanding and wheel construction and so on.

I had come to own some wild turkey feathers and gave one to each. The symbol is the feather along with the quill—take flight, but don't forget to write, I told them. The order of the *Wild Turkey Feather* was born.

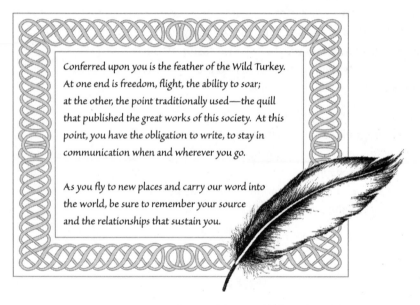

Conferred upon you is the feather of the Wild Turkey. At one end is freedom, flight, the ability to soar; at the other, the point traditionally used—the quill that published the great works of this society. At this point, you have the obligation to write, to stay in communication when and wherever you go.

As you fly to new places and carry our word into the world, be sure to remember your source and the relationships that sustain you.

Endings too often go unrecognized, creating fissures and wounds that lead to angry, frustrated people. Too seldom are these feelings attributed to the real problem—the experience of existential loss.

Sellouts

Several years ago, Seattle's Virginia Mason Clinic was experiencing a difficult problem. Nearly everyone—nurses, staff, administrators, and patients—was complaining about the behavior of the clinic's physicians, but no one could put a finger on what was amiss. At an administrative off-site retreat, discussions revealed to physicians in attendance what was wrong. As a result of cataclysmic changes in health care delivery, many physician groups have been selling their practices to firms or hospitals and becoming employees rather than owners. The partnership had sold their clinical practice to the Virginia Mason hospital. Many of the clinic's physicians felt angry, betrayed, and hurt. But their loss was neither obvious nor officially acknowledged.

As a result of this insight, a planning team put together an off-site retreat for a large group of the physicians. One evening, a fifty-five-minute wake featured humorous skits and physicians singing familiar songs with new lyrics expressing their hurt and anger. The group reacted very emotionally, with both laughter and tears. A week later, the hospital's medical director observed, "Since the retreat, it's like a different group of docs. The event helped launch us into a much needed transition."

Mergers

During the 1980s and 1990s, competition and financial incentives encouraged many business firms to join forces with others and form new organizations. Most of the deals were put together primarily on financial grounds. Deal makers typically ignored or overlooked the human dynamics of combining two separate corporate tribes with unique identities and cultural ways. As a result, many mergers encountered intense difficulties, often failing to accomplish sought-after financial benefits. After Northwest Airlines acquired Republic Airlines, the merged enterprise became known to frequent passengers as Northworst Airlines. Relationships among employees were so frayed and strained that the merger was officially cited by the National Traffic Safety Board as a contributing cause of the fatal crash in Detroit. Only when the company sponsored its "Northbest" program, giving employees a forum to vent their feelings, did the airline's performance improve.

In contrast, Southwest Airlines displayed its artful understanding of the important role of transitional ritual and ceremony when it acquired Utah-based Morris Air. On paper, the proposed merger looked like a sure winner. Morris also flew only 737s and its route structure complemented Southwest's. The cultural compatibility between the two appeared promising. Even so, the more subtle, ephemeral, human aspects of the merger also received ample, sensitive attention.

To christen the merger, the companies got off to a flying start by staging a wedding ceremony in Las Vegas, complete with bride (Morris), bridegroom

(Southwest), ring bearer, flower girl, and spectators. After the ceremony, those in attendance ate wedding cake and drank champagne. In a humorous play on protocol, the bride offered a piece of cake to the bridegroom, pushing it into his face. The groom reciprocated.

The entire event was captured on video. Later, footage was added to the wedding scene showing pilots, flight attendants, baggage handlers, gate agents, and other employees from both companies holding hands and singing together, "We are family, Southwest, Morris, and me." At the video's end, airplanes from each company are shown taking off. A poignant song written by a Southwest employee accompanies the series of takeoffs. "When you take some Morris magic and add some Southwest spirit . . . Take advantage of this great union of two airlines, a new birth."

The event and later video footage juxtapose the joy of a new beginning and the pain of losing old traditions and ways. Together, they jump-started the transition process. As a result, the Morris-Southwest merger was highly successful, with little evidence of the accompanying rancor and bitterness that plagues most merger and acquisition efforts.

Celebrating Change: Navigating the Transition from Old to New

There is little to indicate that downsizing, layoffs, mergers, or business failures will decrease in the years ahead. Rapid change is an inevitable part of life in the twenty-first century. There is no way to avoid the wrenching loss that transitions produce. Transferring employees, renaming business units, merging functions, changing reporting structures—commonplace events in corporate America—all deserve ceremonial recognition bringing closure to the past and generating hope and optimism for the future. Ritual and ceremony provide comfort and healing to help people let go and move on. Coping with change is like performing a trapeze act: You have to release your grip before you can catch the next bar. Properly timed, ritual and ceremony provide a symbolic bridge linking past, present, and future in a continuous, woven, braid-like span.

Chapter 7

Comings and Goings: Personal Transitions

Organizations have revolving doors. People enter and exit all the time across permeable boundaries. Some stay only awhile; others settle down and build a career. Customers and clients come

> When a civilization lacks rites of passage, its soul is sick. The evidence for this sickness is threefold: first, there are no elders; second, the young are violent; third, the adults are bewildered.
>
> —Matthew Fox

and go on a regular basis. Bosses and managers circulate in a musical-chair-like game of promotions and demotions. New hires come aboard, check things out, and decide whether this is a place that fits. Old-timers hang in there, some looking forward to a golden parachute or early retirement. Others leave prematurely. They fall victim to downsizing, rightsizing, restructuring, or whatever label is in vogue to cushion the blow of involuntary layoffs. Scott Adams's *Dilbert* cartoon strip recently captured a tenor of our times:

The boss walks up to an employee and seemingly engages him in playful ritual: "Knock, knock." The employee responds, "Who's there?" The boss drops the bad news: "Not you anymore."

Rites of Entrance and Exit

While the constant flow of clients and customers is expected, the induction and separation of employees and bosses loom as potentially important transitions. Any group when it adds a member or subtracts one becomes a new group in some ways. Almost all significant entrances and exits are symbolically important. As such, they require recognition through ritual and ceremony.

Without proper initiation rites, newcomers never really become full-fledged members of a community. They themselves do not feel completely connected. They are never fully accepted by others. They don't really belong anywhere—either to their past situations or their new circumstances. Without proper closing rites, the departure of veterans leaves a void, an existential wound. Survivors cannot come to terms with the reality that someone is gone and often missed. Those who leave cannot sever the connection or accept their departure. Many of the postwar problems of Vietnam veterans stem from the absence of rites of passage as they departed the war zone and reentered the United States.

As one high-ranking veteran of Vietnam remarked, "We never flipped the switch through a collective rite as we entered the country. And we never flipped the switch when we left the battle zone. That's one reason we're still screwed up.

The following story, as told by a witness, details the rites of passage for several veterans who fought in Desert Storm:

It was like something from the movies. I was on a plane flying from Chicago to Nashville. I was the only paying passenger in first class. In coach, there were several soldiers returning from Saudi Arabia still dressed in their desert khakis. The flight attendant brought them all up to ride in first class. When we got off the plane in Nashville, we walked toward the security checkpoint. All you could see were relatives of the service people—a sea of yellow ribbons. One little girl broke through the security barrier and ran toward us. She jumped into her daddy's arms (he was an army sergeant) and hugged him. The crowd stopped and a hushed silence gripped the setting. Then there was a kind of murmur that grew into a song. No one was leading; it just happened. Suddenly, we were all singing "God Bless America." Not a dry eye in the place.

Throughout history, human societies have created ceremonial events to mark passage from one state to another—the stages and ages of life, as Robert Fulghum calls them. Christenings herald new life. Puberty rites celebrate the transition from childhood to early adulthood. Graduation ceremonies recognize the movement from novice to expert. Marriages take us from being single to matrimonial status. New Year's festivities pass the torch from the old year to the new with appropriate regalia and fanfare. The sentimental singing of "Auld Lang Syne" captures the heart of the occasion: "Should old acquaintance be forgot and never brought to mind?" followed by the noisemakers, fireworks, and toasts to the New Year.

In many of today's organizations, however, transitions are not publicly acknowledged. On their first day, new people arrive, are shown to their offices or cubicles, and get to work. Feeling powerless and vulnerable, they sit at their desks, oblivious to office politics, company history, or even the basic floor plan. At best, retirees get a brief party and a gold watch. People who leave voluntarily or who are terminated too often pack up their things and quietly slip away. Even worse, they are escorted out while their computer access is cut off and the locks are being changed on their doors. The euphemisms of death are used for the involuntarily departed—"It was curtains for her." "He cashed in his chips." "She bit the dust." "He passed on." There is even a colloquial expression in corporate slang that refers to "killing you (or your unit)." Such inattention and negative attention has tremendous social and economic costs. Newcomers need to be welcomed and ushered through initiation rites; those who take their leave should be bid farewell through dignified rites of passage.

Initiation Rituals

As newcomers enter an organization, they typically undergo a series of initiation rites. These experiences impart values and induct initiates into the community. In weak cultures, induction focuses mainly on learning the rules—policies, procedures, and benefits. Cohesive cultures place a premium on learning the ropes— legend, lore, and traditional ways.

Morehouse College

Morehouse College is one of the country's premier black educational institutions. Its distinctive culture envelops prospective students even before they are admitted, as they attend a prospective-student seminar. Then, when freshmen arrive on campus for the beginning of the school year, they go through an experience known as "Welcome to the House" week. Upperclassmen serve as drill instructors, welcoming newcomers to the "House" and indoctrinating them into the widely shared traditions of the college. Freshmen are shown the "Bell"—whose call they must answer whenever it sounds. They are introduced to cultural heroes—graduates who exemplify the college's core values—Martin Luther King, Jr., Thurgood Marshall. Speeches abound with stories and traditions that initiate students into the soul of the institution. Freshmen are randomly paired with "sisters" from Spellman College—a nearby institution for African-American females. In the ceremony, they are asked to honor and respect those of the opposite gender.

A walk around the Morehouse campus demonstrates the power of the early socialization experience. Everyone knows what the institution stands for and what is expected of them during their stay and after graduation. Through this powerful socialization experience, the values of Morehouse are permanently etched in the hearts and minds of students.

Data General's Eagle Group

Initiation into a corporate culture can also begin during the interview process. It is not always pleasant, however, or without manipulation. It sometimes takes the intense form of hazing. In *The Soul of a New Machine*, Tracy Kidder describes the success of Data General's Eagle Group in designing a state-of-the-art new computer. Kidder credits the act of "signing up," the group's distinctive hazing rite, as one of the factors in creating a committed and cohesive team culture. "Signing up" took place in an interview with one of the Eagle Group's leaders and is described in the following passage from his book. (In parentheses are the leader's thoughts about what he is doing.)

> "Well," says Alsing [the group's leader] "we're building this machine that's way out in front in technology. We're gonna design all new hardware and tools. ("*I'm trying to give him [the new recruit] a sense of 'Hey, you've finally found in a big company, a place where people are really doing the next thing.'*") Do you like the sound of that?" asks Alsing.
>
> "Oh yeah," says the recruit.
>
> ("*Now I tell him the bad news.*")
>
> "It's gonna be tough," says Alsing. "If we hired you, you'd be working with a bunch of cynics and egotists and it'd be hard to keep up with them."
>
> "That doesn't scare me," says the recruit.
>
> "There's a lot of fast people in this group," Alsing goes on. "It's gonna be a real hard job with a lot of long hours. And I mean *long* hours."
>
> "No," says the recruit, in words more or less like these. "That's what I want to do, get in on the ground floor of a new architecture. I want to do a big machine. I want to be where the action is."
>
> "Well," says Alsing, pulling a long face. "We can only let in the best of this year's graduates. We've already let in some awfully fast people. We'll have to let you know."
>
> ("*We tell him that we only let in the best. Then we let him in.*")
>
> "I don't know," said Alsing, after it was all done. "It was kind of like recruiting for a suicide mission. You're gonna die, but you're gonna die in glory" (pp. 65–66).

While some might find this kind of initiation distasteful, "signing up" gave prospective recruits a feeling for the project's culture. The Eagle Group was an intense, all-encompassing place where people devoted their lives to building a new machine. They succeeded, in part, because the group's ways were etched into new recruits from day one.

Nordstrom Department Stores

Nordstrom Department Stores is a widely known example of just how customer friendly a retail business can be. There are many reasons why. One is how new employees are indoctrinated into the company's ways. In a small training room located in a Seattle office building, newcomers to Nordstrom quickly learn cultural values. Aspiring "Nordies" meet the company's pantheon of heroes and heroines, who embody and represent the Nordstrom mystique, and they are steeped in the history and traditions of one of the most successful retail companies in America. Robert Spector and Patrick D. McCarthy, in their book *The Nordstrom Way*, describe the training room.

> One wall represents history, with a grainy, ninety-year-old picture of the original founders and partners, Carl F. Wallin and John W. Nordstrom, proudly standing outside their first tiny shoe store. . . . At the opposite end of the room, functioning as a counterpoint, are individual formal portraits of the four current co-chairmen. . . . Displayed on the back wall are photographs of the company's other officers. . . . Dispersed around the room are several three-foot by two-foot placards that feature head shots of outstanding employees and details of their career paths up the Nordstrom "Pyramid of Success" to the position of store manager (pp.16–17).

In an intense, carefully planned experience, newcomers to Nordstrom learn the company's history, values, and cardinal rule. Written on a five-by-eight inch gray card—the Nordstrom Employee Handbook—the rule says:

> **Welcome to Nordstrom**
>
> We're glad to have you with our Company. Our number one goal is to provide outstanding customer service. Set both your personal and professional goals high. We have great confidence in your ability to achieve them.
>
> **Nordstrom Rules:**
>
> Rule #1. Use your good judgment in all situations.
> There will be no additional rules. Please feel free to ask your department manager, store manager, or division general manager any question at any time. (pp. 15–16).

For some, the training event will imprint permanently what it takes to succeed, heading them for a long-term career with the company. For others, the strong socialization pressures may quickly let them know that Nordstrom is not for them.

Playfair's Circle of Secrets

Why wait until someone retires to have a party? Why not give a new employee an immediate welcome and induction into the team? This was Playfair's intention when they created a welcoming ritual called Circle of Secrets, described in CEO Matt Weinstein's book, *Managing to Have Fun*.

> We send employees flowers on the first day of work, and hold an elaborate welcoming ceremony during their first staff retreat. In the ritual, we make the new employee the "Keeper of Secrets." We make ourselves vulnerable to them by giving them some "superhuman power" over us. The members of the company stand in a big circle around which the new hire is led, blindfolded, from one person to the next. Each person whispers

a secret about him or herself that no one else knows. A roll of crepe paper marks the route of their journey, so that members of the team will pass by and see the physical reminder of the ritual.

All of Playfair's welcoming rituals use the elements of the Circle of Secrets: playful gestures of equality and accommodation that say, "You are a valuable member of this team. You may be a new hire, but you're not alone. There is a lot of support for you here. We welcome you. This is a safe place to play" (pp. 167–69).

Whatever form initiation takes, most successful American businesses acculturate new members into the fold. Socialization is never left to chance. Newcomers quickly learn the company's history, values, and ways. Another example is Disney; all new hires go through an intensive "Traditions" course where they learn the company's distinctive language and culture. The orientation is taught entirely by current job incumbents, who tell stories that emphasize the qualities Disney expects and polishes in its people.

Without intense induction rituals and ceremonies, newcomers never learn their place and veterans miss an opportunity to shape recruits into the desired corporate mold. Following is a clear statement of the feelings of a group of graduate students who, well into their careers, were finally exposed to their university's history and traditions:

> We feel cheated. We never heard any of this stuff before. We just arrived and started classes. As a result, we've had a mechanical connection with the place. We do what we're told; we get our diploma. Today, as we walked the grounds with our elders and heard the stories, we could feel our feet sinking into the sacred soil. Our hearts were touched by the spirit of this place. We now feel an organic attachment we never experienced before.

Rituals of induction and incorporation weave newcomers into the culture's tapestry. Without robust initiation rites, people entering an organization are shut off from its history, isolated from its veterans, and oblivious to its cultural values and ways. As a result, new arrivals are left to fend for themselves, and too often they founder, fail, or leave.

Separation Rites

Retirement, retrenchment, reassignment, resignation—even promotion—take people away from their current place of work or position to pursue other options. Too often, taking one's leave means walking away with a minimal amount of fanfare or flair. This usually has its costs: Dull departures short-circuit closure and dampen community spirit. Leaving is a loss-experience that has an impact on those who remain as well as on those who leave. Culturally aware organizations invent ways to ease the pain of departure, paving the way for a positive transition.

In *Life and Work*, James Autry describes a distinctive twist given to a ceremony honoring those with corporate longevity. The twist transformed a drab, somber retirement event into a robust, memorable, lively ceremony. A company executive presented the customary gold watch to a twenty-year honoree following the traditional script, but then ad-libbed: "Tony, it took you twenty years to develop a green thumb, but after only three weeks with this cheap watch, you'll have a green wrist" (p. 26). Everyone, including Tony, burst into raucous laughter.

Now the irreverent tone of retirement parties has become a company tradition. As Autry himself received his own gold watch, he commented on the wisdom of adding more vice presidents to the executive team at a time when the malfunctioning air conditioning at headquarters was not being fixed because of a tight budget: "I sang a carol to the tune of 'The Twelve Days of Christmas' with the closing line, 'Give us fewer vice presidents and more air conditioning'" (pp. 26–27).

Lessons from the U.S. Military

The U.S. military has learned that poignant succession ceremonies serve several important purposes: They honor the departing commander, welcome and christen the incoming replacement, and provide the entire unit with a vibrant, emotionally charged, public opportunity to say "good-bye and hello." Experience has taught the military that a change of command requires appropriate pomp and circumstance. Without it, outgoing commanders, as well as the unit's remaining officers and enlisted personnel, have trouble letting go, and incoming commanders find it difficult to establish their authority and gain the loyalty and commitment of the troops.

When General Hoar succeeded General Schwarzkopf as commander of Central Command, the American public witnessed a striking example of what a successful transition ritual looks like. Officials and their families—Schwarzkopf, Hoar, Cheney, and Powell—gathered before the official event in an informal setting. They were served coffee and refreshments, and they greeted ambassadors and high-ranking military officers from twenty-five coalition countries from across the world. They were then transported to the ceremony in separate vehicles, arriving in order of rank before an assembly of the Central Command's troops, close relatives, and other spectators.

Following an age-old, traditional script, the ceremony unfolded. Introductions kicked off the event, followed by a cannon salute. Schwarzkopf and Hoar inspected the troops against the backdrop of a march played by a military band. After the singing of the national anthem, the command's flag was passed from Schwarzkopf to Hoar through their superior, Defense Secretary Cheney. Schwarzkopf's career was then recounted with special reference to his performance in Desert Storm.

Schwarzkopf gave his farewell address. He told his troops, "I shall always love you and will never, ever, ever forget you." He was moved to tears as were nearly all in attendance. Hoar delivered his acceptance speech. The audience sang "Amazing Grace." The troops passed in review. A military band played the "Armed Service Medley," anthems of the Army, Air Force, Navy, Marines, and Coast Guard. The entire assembly sang "Auld Lang Syne."

This transition event accomplished its dual purposes: a departing hero appropriately acknowledged and a new commander officially recognized. The king is dead; long live the king: An outgoing person recognized and revered; his incoming replacement given the official mantle of authority in a public forum.

While military changes of command generally go by the book, ceremonies for those retiring from the armed services offer more latitude in choosing a script. The same attention to detail, level of ceremonial flair, and reverence for the spirit of the occasion, however, is manifest. Lt. Colonel Sandra Murray's retirement from the U.S. Air Force provides a vivid example. In an interview with the authors, she obviously sensed the true meaning of the event:

> A retirement is a cross between a wedding (the roles), a funeral (the emotions), and a graduation (presents and celebration). It can be personalized with an entire day of festivities and a public celebration, or it can be minimized, that is, just read the

retirement certificate in the commander's office and go home. I chose to celebrate. . . . For me, knowing it was coming was part of processing—it started to prepare me for leaving prior to the event.

A team from Wright-Patterson Medical Center USAF was put in charge of Lt. Colonel Murray's retirement event, and they sought out her desires. Her wishes shaped every detail of the official ceremonial protocol: who would officiate, who would carry the pillow holding the medals and awards, who would serve as ushers, who would handle the guest book, whether an honor guard would bring in and place the flags, what music would be played.

On the day of the event, her family arrived and was escorted by military representatives into a private, nicely decorated room. As the ceremony began, family members were escorted to the front of the gathering, accompanied by soft music.

The emcee, also known as the retiring officer, is the commander of the retirement event. He or she announces who the retiree is and then walks down the aisle with the retiree. A four-person honor guard follows: one person in front and one behind, each with mock rifles, and two in the middle with flags. Everyone stands up for the national anthem.

> In my case, the retiring officer called me up and then awards and certificates were given—National Defense, Meritorious Service, medals, and so on. They read my accomplishments and gave me my retirement certificate signed by the president. Then there was a place in the program to recognize the contributions of the spouse to the retiree's career. Typically, flowers are given, as it is a predominantly male field and spouses are usually female; but I chose to change tradition and present a plaque to my husband, Byron, as a token of my deep appreciation. I stood while the commander made a speech making me feel I had been important to others throughout my career. He then asked if others wanted to speak.

Several of Lt. Colonel Murray's friends paid tribute to her unique qualities and accomplishments. Their testimony was followed by a videotape of the surgeon general of the Air Force offering comments on her distinguished career.

Now it was my turn to talk. I had a choice; I could say what was expected—a formula speech—or I could be authentic—show the emotion I was feeling. I chose the latter. I told those attending that it was their job to pass me tissue—I think that helped me. It allowed us all to be emotional together. I think I said more thank yous for what I had learned. I talked about the role of family in preparing me and asked them to come up to be presented flowers. I talked about the quality of friends' unselfish sharing and their courage to be different. I thanked my office and honored the Team of All Teams: These are the people who began the journey with me at Wright Patterson (they were all there and you know, the military does not pay for travel for this, although they do give special leave). Many surprised me by showing up. I had never been so touched in all of my life. I broke tradition and asked my team to come up for pictures.

Many humdrum retirement events are staged out of necessity; people trudge mindlessly through the motions. In contrast, this event has special style and character. It ties past, present, and future together. It includes members of the family. It oozes with symbols and values. It elicits comments on the departing person's career from a number of different sources. It features music and flowers. It gives the retirees a special place in the limelight and the chance to offer a parting silhouette. It is an intensely emotional event. As a result of all this, it works. It paves the way for a successful transition for both the retiree and those who remain. Lt. Colonel Murray also had the following to say:

Part of what I'd struggled with as I prepared to retire was the pain of leaving the group. I'm sure many feel this as they retire, but work hard to hide their pain and emotion. It's so hard to leave and yet so right and so joyful. I realized I would never belong in the same way; I would forever be on the outside looking in. I felt I was losing so much. It caused me to evaluate losing versus gaining. I was afraid of losing my coworkers as friends. But in seeing everyone there, I realized I could move on without losing my friends.

> There wasn't a dry eye among us. They all stood up and clapped. We walked out to the Air Force song, "Off we go, into the wild, blue yonder . . ."

In too many companies, departures, retirements, and management successions do not receive this kind of attention or ceremonial recognition. People move over, out, or up without rituals or ceremonies to pave the way for a successful transition.

Involuntary Exits

But what should be protocol when people are downsized, dumped, or demoted? In the United States, for example, thousands of jobs have or are being sacrificed to cut costs and add more heft to the bottom line. Many of those terminated have invested years in a career they believed was full of payoff and promise. In a flash, their long-term hopes and dreams abruptly come to an end. Typically, under such circumstances, people leave with little ceremonial recognition. No one knows what to do or how to behave. But ritual and ceremony are even more crucial when people leave without choice than when the exit is voluntary. Transition rites not only confer dignity and grace upon the departing person, they also provide comfort and closure for those who remain. Meaningful rituals create collective remembrance, a reminder that those who depart involuntarily still leave their mark.

To illustrate, in a large multinational company, a long-term veteran manager was let go. Although John Martin had for many years been a productive member of the management group, shifts in the company's competitive position demanded radical cost-cutting at all levels. One of the most difficult aspects of the forced separation was John's informal role as a mentor to aspiring leaders. Many of the company's managerial ranks were staffed with people John had personally coached and nurtured.

Despite universal appeal for a recognition event, the company's managing director vetoed the idea. In his mind, the circumstances of John's termination did not warrant public celebration. Better he just leave the company as quietly as possible. On John's last day, a group of his loyal followers had secretly planned a parting event. As John packed up his things and made his way to the headquarter's foyer, a large group awaited with food and flowers. They toasted John and told stories about his behind-the-scenes influence. As the festivities wound down, John was escorted to the front door. When he looked down toward the parking lot, the stone walkway was flanked on both sides with individuals he had mentored over the years, each holding a small evergreen tree.

As John passed in review, each person hugged him or shook his hand. As he moved along, the evergreens were planted, a living tribute to a man who had prepared the ground for so many people to grow and flourish. The event allowed John some dignity and grace in a less-than-favorable departure. It also gave others a chance to say thank you and to symbolize his role in their growth and development. Both John and the company's workforce were able to let go and move on—with a lasting commemorative of his contributions to the company.

Personal Transition in a Time of Disruptive Change

The ebb and flow of people entering and leaving organizations will continue to intensify in the years ahead. Unless these comings and goings are marked with ritual and ceremony, organizations will become fragmented and empty. People will not be able to either latch on or let go. Influence will be exercised by departed ghosts; new arrivals will be resented and shunned.

Rites of initiation and termination offer powerful opportunities for organizations to achieve closure and become whole, to benefit rather than suffer from entrances and exits. Time, attention, and resources assigned to designing appropriate transition events pay substantial dividends over the long haul in building a cohesive work community. Shortchanging or overlooking transitions undermines commitment and loyalty, robbing an organization of its competitive edge.

Chapter 8

Celebration for Others: Workplace Altruism

To this point, we have emphasized celebrations aimed at an organization's internal triumphs, travails, and transitions. But just as Buddhist prayer takes two forms—inward focus and outward action—so too can corporate ritual and ceremony. Doing good for others in the world is a powerful mobilizer of collective energy, and there are hundreds of ways in which people can celebrate themselves and their place of work by exuding kindness for those who need a boost in life. Pulling together to help others strengthens the cultural bonds of the workplace. When donations of time, money, and

> We vow to bring joy to one person in the morning and to ease the pain of one person in the afternoon.
>
> We know that the happiness of others is indeed our own happiness, and we vow to practice joy on the path of service.
>
> We know that every word, every look, every smile can bring happiness to another person.
>
> We know that if we practice wholeheartedly, then we ourselves become an inexhaustible source of peace and joy for our clients, our customers, our coworkers, our family, and our friends.
>
> —Bodhisattva Samantabhadra

other resources come from a widely shared feeling of making a difference, corporate benefits are as great as the charitable payoff to beneficiaries. External recipients of corporate kindness campaigns include clients or customers, shareholders, various local community groups, and the wider society.

The Collective Joy of Helping Others

The pleasure that people experience when they help others is a natural motivator. Most of us feel good knowing we eased someone's pain or brightened someone's day. Serving the collective good is most always a popular theme for stimulating celebration. Responding to national crises like the Oklahoma bombing, volunteering for local charities like United Way, even taking up a collection for a fellow employee or customer in need gives people a feeling of making a difference. Putting community interests before one's own interest cleanses the soul and buoys our sense of altruism. Helping others elevates the self and summons up the individual connection to the common good that lurks in the heart of almost everyone.

Many corporations celebrate by doing something special for a good cause, some more visibly than others. Examples of employee volunteerism include donating time to Habitat for Humanity or Ronald McDonald Houses, helping the homeless, raising money for charity, serving as mentors for young people or companions for old people, adopting families or schools. Companies also reach out to the community by sharing facilities or resources, donating company products and services to those in need, or giving employees time off for doing charitable deeds. Some examples of contemporary corporate kindness programs are presented in table 2, but it is only a sampling. Thanks in part to a book by Conari Press, *Random Acts of Kindness*, it is possible to identify an even wider range of companies that have begun kindness campaigns.

One example of a kindness campaign is Playfair's New Student Orientation program, described by Matt Weinstein in *Managing to Have Fun*. Under this program, Playfair staff have traveled to more than three hundred college and university campuses, campaigning for efforts to spread kindness. They bring freshmen together in groups of twelve and challenge them to come up with one kind act they can perform in the coming week. Their commitment gels group unity and identity. Subsequently, compassionate acts flow easily to others. Following are some examples of what the students come up with:

★ Serenade the occupants of the senior citizen center.

★ Make a meal you can bring to the homeless people in the area.

★ Help the man with eighteen stray cats take care of them for a week.

★ Volunteer to work together at a battered women's shelter.

Joining Forces to Promote Social Change

People enjoy volunteering and would probably do more of it if companies encouraged community participation as part of corporate responsibility. What if all organizations convened employees for the combined purposes of celebrating and doing good for others? This could serve as a valuable rallying point for celebration and a more effective way to mobilize collective energy than merely extracting monetary donations from individuals. It would also infuse communities with welcome charitable acts.

According to an April 22, 1997, article in USA *Today*, a USA *Today*/CNN/ Gallup Poll survey showed that 65 percent of employees volunteered in the last year, 20 percent frequently. Eight out of ten of those surveyed said they would be more likely to volunteer if their companies recognized their volunteer work by providing paid time off to do it; only 14 percent have that paid time off now. It's not just the time off that provides the motivation, it's the fact that the company values service to others. Let's look at some examples of what can happen when an organization rallies employees behind important social causes.

The Body Shop

Anita Roddick, CEO of The Body Shop, strongly advocates business as a powerful force for positive social change. In *Anita Roddick Speaks Out on "Spirituality and Service,"* she reminds us that corporations were invented to serve people and society. Business leaders, therefore, have a moral obligation to invest companies with a

COMPANY	ACTS
Kimberly-Clark Corp.	will spend $2 million and offer thousands of employees to help build playgrounds in 30 needy communities in 1997.*
Blue Cross Blue Shield	will offer free health coverage to 250,000 children whose parents can't afford insurance and don't qualify for Medicaid.
Coca-Cola	will give $50 million, bringing its total commitment to $100 million, to recruit at-risk teens to serve as mentors and tutors for elementary school children in 90 schools.
IBM	will give $10 million by the year 2000 to provide technology and technical services to more than 2,500 nonprofit groups.
Time Warner	will give 1 million employee volunteer hours for literacy tutoring by the year 2000.*
KPMG Peat Marwick	will give 20,000 employees a paid day off each year to do community service.*
Timberland	will give every employee 40 hours a year to do volunteer work.*
COMCAST	will provide 1 million hours of free high-speed Internet access to more than 250 public libraries in 20 states.
Eli Lilly	will offer 80,000 volunteer hours and give more than $13 million in cash and products to a variety of volunteer groups.*
Federated Department Stores	will give 50,000 hours of employee volunteer time for tutoring and mentoring.*
General Mills	will give $2.1 million for scholarships for troubled kids.
MCI	will give $1.1 million to help train kids on the Internet.
Nationsbank	will establish 250 "Make a Difference Centers" to provide after-school programs for 250,000 children by the year 2000.*

Table 2. Organizations and Their Kindness Campaigns (continued on next page)

COMPANY	ACTS
Pfizer	will give $5 million in medicine and grants to community health centers.
K-Mart	will give $50 million for drug education and will offer 2,150 of its stores as after-school "safe havens" for kids.*
Brinks Home Security	will give each of its 2,000 employees one day off with pay each year to volunteer. It will also provide a six-week course on personal safety twice a year to children at 150 Boys & Girls Clubs.*
LensCrafters	will give 1 million disadvantaged children free vision care by 2003.
Ronald McDonald House	will give $100 million to prevent child abuse and teen suicide.
NFL Players Association	will recruit retired and active NFL players to act as mentors for Native American teenagers.*
Honeywell	will mobilize 8,000 employees to mentor kids and recruit 4,000 volunteers to help build affordable housing for low-income families.*
American Booksellers Assoc.	will recruit 50,000 employees and customers to volunteer as reading tutors.*
Southwest Airlines	will start an "Adopt a Pilot" program in which pilots will teach school children the value of math and science in aviation.*
Walt Disney Co.	will contribute 1 million employee volunteer hours through the year 2000.*
Dayton Hudson Stores	will commit to a "weekend of giving" each year for three years. Employees will encourage young people to do volunteer work.*
Scholastic Books	will donate 1 million books to help ensure that every child can read by third grade.

* Campaign involves employees.

Source: "Leading Corporations Commit to Charitable Causes," USA *Today* 22 April 1997, 2A.

higher purpose, to champion efforts for promoting human good. She herself exemplifies this call to moral leadership by blending spirituality and service into the official mission of The Body Shop. She wants a workplace where "you can bring your heart to work with you" (p. 3). She thinks it is important for employees to know that they are extremely powerful and highly capable of harnessing their energies to serve noble purposes.

As one example, pictures of missing persons are posted on the sides of their transport trucks. The vehicles serve as moving billboards to widen the scope of the search process. When a missing person is located, The Body Shop employees gather to celebrate. Other poignant political and social messages are broadcast as the trucks go about their business: "If you think you're too small to make a difference, you've never been in bed with a mosquito," or "You think education's expensive? Try ignorance." Employees also take what the company calls externships; they go together on social missions such as painting an orphanage in Rumania or working with AIDS-infected babies. "When a young woman comes back from such a project with a light in her eyes and proclaims, 'This is the real me!'—take heed, for she is dreaming of noble purposes not a moisture cream," says Anita. "When you do this sort of work, it absolutely brings a spiritual dimension to the workplace" (p. 8).

Iris Arc Crystal

The following story is taken from *Chicken Soup for the Soul at Work*:

> Iris Arc Crystal experienced a lull in business and the company had only enough work for four days a week. Rather than letting 20 percent of employees go or sending everyone home one day a week, they decided to take Fridays to do service projects in Santa Barbara. Cleaning and painting houses, setting up a bleacher for the riding academy for physically challenged, they had a lot of fun together and ended up with the name The Arc Angels. A cofounder of the firm wrote, "In addition to the good feelings that came from helping out others, the good feelings we shared as employees of a company that cared for both its employees and the community went a long way toward creating a work atmosphere that was a joy to be part of" (pp. 40–41).

Dayton Hudson

For fifty years, Dayton Hudson has given 5 percent of its taxable income to support nonprofit organizations. To celebrate its fiftieth year in 1996, the company initiated the "50 Acts of Giving" program, whereby stores could select opportunities and recruit volunteers for projects like neighborhood cleanups or food drives. Through this program, Dayton Hudson hoped to reinvest more than $23 million in the local communities it serves.

Saturn Retailers

Several years ago, the city of Columbia, Tennessee, brought in a group of consultants headed by Barry Segal and Bob Leathers to design a playground for the community's young people. Kids' ideas were solicited to guide the design. Adult volunteers, many from Saturn's Spring Hill plant, were responsible for the construction. The project was on a tight deadline. Unexpected difficulties and inclement weather stalled the process. With the deadline approaching, the call went out for more help and was answered by Saturn retailers. From all over the Southeast, volunteer retailers were bused into the location. They joined hundreds of other volunteers who swarmed—digging, hammering, hauling, and sawing—to finish the project on time. The delight on the children's faces as they clambered over the playground of their dreams was the ultimate reward.

Doing good for others bonds employees together in the common purpose of serving humanity. The experience of making a difference and the pleasure of giving something back to the local community pays huge dividends to the company in psychological, cultural, and therefore financial ways. The energy generated by selfless acts builds a culture of giving of oneself. And the unity of common purpose creates alignment.

Celebrating Clients and Customers

Both clients and customers love communication and they appreciate being included in ritual and ceremony, as the following stories illustrate.

Liquid Courage

The idea of celebrating customers spawns a regular ritual for Iliad, Inc., a music production firm in Nashville, Tennessee. Iliad holds a weekly Thursday afternoon champagne event and invites all employees, suppliers, clients, and friends to participate. Dubbed "Liquid Courage" by Iliad's owner, Paul Whitehead, "This is the place where new ideas come forth and we celebrate who we are. Clients see us in a disarmed environment—not negotiating or selling."

The ceremony starts with the 4:28 two-minute warning, followed by the 4:30 popping of the cork. One person is chosen as the lead corker for the day and shoots the top as far as possible down the ninety-foot hallway. Then, with the imbibing of "liquid courage," the telling of stories and conviviality begins. "This ongoing storytelling, including old retold stories, allows the culture to be spread across the entire organization," says Whitehead.

The result? Loyal clients, a family feeling, and an open and free environment where individuals step forth to share their good ideas as well as their tragedies. According to Whitehead,

> The real heroes in our business are the buyers who stayed late, the public relations people who wrote the marketing plan that launched our ideas, the artist who did the graphics, the guy who scheduled the truck. These are not the senior vice presidents; these are the line workers who live in mega-corporations where their worth is downplayed. We find and embrace them, building relationships that will make us all successful. We engage our customers in a major, single focus—we create an opportunity to recognize both the client and ourselves for value.

One of Iliad's altruistic ceremonies was an elegant dinner and tribute to a client who supported the production of five classical albums that became platinum (over one million sold—a distinction for only twelve classical albums). Representatives from all aspects of the production, such as the London Symphony Orchestra, gave stirring speeches honoring the client; then framed platinum CDs were conferred. As the media looked on, every person who touched the project was wined, dined, and honored. The evening evoked the feeling of the music—elegant, romantic, beautiful. To this day, the customer calls Iliad the jewel in their crown.

Highlighting Partnership with Customers

We have already mentioned Wal-Mart's flair for celebrating employees and shareholders. The following story, told by Betty Sanders in *Fabled Service*, illustrates how the same convivial spirit is extended to its customers.

Four thousand people carpooled, bused, and flew to the Wal-Mart headquarters in Bentonville, Arkansas. It was a mixed bag of attendees: Every Wal-Mart associate who served in Desert Storm was there, but the bulk of the crowd was made up of vendors, customers, and stockholder representatives selected from every store in the company.

> As the field house filled to capacity and then well beyond, Mr. Sam Walton became concerned that some of the associates had to stand. What did the wealthiest man in America and CEO of the world's most successful retail company do? He invited those standing to come forward and sit on the stage. A couple hundred of them bashfully responded. After their initial embarrassment, they became caught up in the spirit of the event and became the chorus for all the cheering that was coming from Sam.
>
> The accolades continued. Vendors were thanked and the most successful partnerships were highlighted. Of particular importance were those manufacturers who had worked with Wal-Mart to keep or create jobs in the United States. Shareholders were thanked for their confidence and stock analysts for their shrewd support. . . . Most of all, this meeting was a celebration of customers. The tribute focused on how everyone had helped Wal-Mart delight more customers than anyone else in history (pp. 37–39).

Dealers as Customers

The ultimate business customer is not always the most immediate one. Patsy Bruce of Nashville's Events Unlimited talks about the importance of dealers as customers:

> Manufacturers of products, particularly cars, do not really sell to the public. They sell to the car dealers. . . . Honda brings all the dealers, their wives, and their general managers together and

> shows them the new product in a wonderful environment. . . .
> They are saying to the dealers, "By gosh, we think a lot of you.
> We think you're great guys." They entertain the heck out of them
> and the next morning show them the new product. They show
> them the new advertising campaign. The dealers go away real
> pumped, ready to sell that new car to the ultimate customer.

Bruce and her colleagues have designed celebrations for Honda dealers for the past ten years. They are lavish events, intended to produce, as one Honda dealer put it, "motivating memories that last a lifetime." The dealers have been feted in the New Orleans Superdome, where a small-scale replica of the French Quarter, complete with buildings, restaurants, and backdrop, had been constructed. When the company was twenty years old, Events Unlimited designed a corporate rodeo. The event drew an analogy between the development of American Honda and the development of the American West and the cowboy—America's only white knight. "When the cowboy rode into the arena, everybody bought into it. They were standing on their chairs screaming because they got the analogy."

Internal Customers

All celebrations of others do not have to be directed to customers outside an organization. Employees and coworkers are internal customers who also some- times need a helping hand. Who has not experienced empathy for a coworker who was undergoing tough times and watched him or her suffer silently on the job. In *Care Packages*, Barbara Glanz relays a story from Catherine Angeli, the manager of the Gogebic and Iron County offices of the Michigan Department of Social Ser- vices (DSS).

> An employee's seven-year-old son was terminally ill with cancer
> and his mom wanted to stay home with him during his last
> days, but she did not have enough vacation time left. A number
> of her coworkers wanted to donate some of their leave time to
> her, so a policy was created that allowed any DSS employee to
> donate up to 240 hours. Several different offices called with
> donated hours and the calls were still coming in well after the
> maximum had been donated (p. 173).

The Spirit of Reciprocity

Whoever the prime beneficiaries happen to be, ceremonial spirit is contagious. When you are celebrated, you want to give something in return—in the spirit of reciprocity. Customers often turn things around and celebrate their benefactors. They do so in inventive and special ways.

Consider the moving story of a patient-made quilt given to a hospital's caregivers. The quilt became the inspiration for a celebration planned by patients and families who had survived cancer with the help of employees of the Washington Cancer Institute at Washington Hospital Center (WHC). They wanted to give something in return for the compassionate care they had received from the institute's staff. Chris Vinh, an assistant vice president of WHC and a quilter, talked to us about the event.

The common thread of cancer survival at our hospital is healing hands and hearts—the theme for our quilts. Every block of the quilt could mean anything to a survivor or their family, as long as they used the hands and hearts symbols. The hands could be those of God, a doctor, a nurse, a pastor, members of their family, church, or support group, or support-group children. The hearts could be someone else's or their own being touched by others. One patient, an eight-year survivor, expressed her gratitude using the hands and hearts of the doctor and of her family; she made a second square with hands holding a broken heart together for a friend who had passed away. Another patient had three or four doctors hands with the script, "Thank you for my

life." Then there was a heart with God's hands at the top and the patient's hands offering it up from below. Another expressed the joy of survival through butterflies: "Every time you see a butterfly, think of me."

The quilts were hung ceremoniously on Cancer Survivors Day in June 1997. According to Chris, the event unfolded better than expected: The turnout was great and the hands and hearts wove everything together. The quilts were blessed by a rabbi, a priest, and a Baptist preacher. The speakers were a survivor, a mother of a deceased survivor, a health-care provider (whose hands were portrayed in many quilt squares), and a quilter (Chris). Most all were survivors themselves. Even the musicians were relatives of survivors, donating their time. Participants wore buttons with the number of years of survival marked. At one point, survivors stood and held hands—everyone was touched by someone. Honors and recognitions were made, so that ultimately everyone was recognized. Finally, the closing, "Wind Beneath My Wings," was sung a capella by a woman who has suffered recurrent bouts of breast cancer—you can rise above anything.

There is something special about a quilt as a focal point of celebration. Many hands, many ideas come together artistically in a heart-felt symbol of warmth and comfort. Historically, quilting bees have brought women together in a communal enterprise. The AIDS quilt has traveled the country, blanketing many miles and touching many hearts. Drawing on such well-known examples, patients of the Washington Cancer Institute produced a lasting and visible way to express to staff members what their compassionate care really meant.

Doing Good in the World

In creating ceremonial occasions for community or customers, corporations nourish their own collective spirit. Workplace altruism is not an after-hours enterprise to be tacked on with little thought. Good deeds call attention to the social purpose of organizations—to do good in the world. There is no limit to the amount of good corporations can do by giving those in need a boost. What greater purpose can there be for meaningful celebration?

Chapter 9

Play at Work: Fun Ignites Energy

Years ago, Johan Huizinga wrote *Homo Ludens*, a book capturing the innate urge of people to engage in playful activity. To Huizinga, play is

> **Life should be lived as play.**
>
> —Plato

a free activity standing quite consciously outside "ordinary" life as not being serious, but at the same time absorbing the player intensely and utterly. It is an activity connected with no material interest, and no profit can be gained by it (p. 13).

While no profit may be extracted directly from play, its indirect benefits can yield handsome dividends. Substituting more fanciful rules and eliminating material goals offers people opportunities to move outside formal boundaries, create novel ideas, spin new visions, form better relationships, blow off a little steam, and just have some fun together. Too often in today's organizations, deadlines and demands eclipse opportunities for play at work. In some companies, taking time from pressing tasks and money matters seems like a senseless waste, a sluggish drag on productivity, and a sucking drain on profits. For many people, work has nothing to do with play. A job becomes eight hours or more of daily drudgery.

Not so with exemplary companies that excel at creating multiple opportunities to play, celebrate, and have a little fun. Their aim is to enhance relationships, build feelings of team spirit, nourish a sense of community, and release the corporate spirit. There is no other official agenda or mandate. We call it "Joy for Joy's Sake." In researching this book, certain companies repeatedly surfaced as models for embracing the concept of playing at work, infusing the workplace with frolic and fun.

Kingpins of Play at Work

Take, for example, NRDC, the telephone repair company mentioned earlier that gleefully orchestrated its transformation from a bankrupt to an excellent operation by instituting ample opportunities to play. Some examples are Rock and Roll Day, a backyard barbecue and dance with booming rock and roll music for which employees formed their own NRDC Band to add local talent to the event's entertainment pool; and Team Day, which features competition within and among groups in such outrageous events as tricycle races. On Elvis Day, CEO Burgess Oliver plays Elvis; at Christmas, he dresses up as Santa; and on Halloween, he dons whatever is handy. Because NRDC's "Let's Party" attitude has paid off, there is now something fun going on every month.

Southwest Airlines, featured throughout this book, is the epitome of a party community. Celebration is Southwest's way of life and is almost always done up right. The employees' hard work and exuberant play attitudes operate hand in hand to create a joyful work environment. The zest and vitality of Southwest's workforce are widely renowned and often imitated. Pep rallies are the substance of culture exchange meetings, one of many ways of keeping the Southwest spirit alive. People come together periodically in balloon-festooned hangars to spend a day exchanging ideas and working up enthusiasm.

Walt Disney Company is also a model of a fun-filled, service-oriented culture. Customer service is well taught, joyfully practiced, and passionately demonstrated. Disney's Cast Activities is a department dedicated solely to providing services and fun functions for employees. In "How Disney Keeps Ideas Coming" in the April 1, 1996, issue of *Fortune* magazine, Joe McGowan points out that in addition to tangible perks, like a company store, the Cast Activities group hosts after-hours scavenger hunts; canoe races around Tom Sawyer's island; volleyball, softball, and basketball leagues; and an annual picnic featuring relay races and obstacle courses. The playful aim is to enhance team feeling and enthusiasm and to have fun. Michael Eisner, chairman and CEO of Disney, plays Ping-Pong with employees at lunch time. Disney's adapted version of The Gong Show gets everyone at corporate together three times a year to generate new ideas. The top four executives sit at a table in the middle of a large room as people pitch their ideas. They have fun and learn quickly that no matter how good, bad, or indifferent the idea, it can be playfully expressed, thoughtfully considered, and occasionally accepted.

Ben & Jerry's Ice Cream has a permanent committee called the Joy Gang. The committee's job is to plan fun activities for employees by (1) making Joy Grants of up to $500 for gleeful ideas that might create joy in a work space; (2) creating permanent spontaneity through regular outlandish surprises; and (3) creating preplanned contests and events, such as "Clash Dressing Day." (Weinstein 1996, 130–32).

As a final example, Playfair has excelled for twenty years as a laboratory for developing fun-centered management skills. Like all good trainers, they use themselves as guinea pigs to test playful new activities. Fun and play are centerpieces of the way they themselves do business, and they take pride in teaching others the art of "practicing joy on the path of service." In working with client companies, they recognize that cultivating a playful attitude often requires a cultural transformation that allows play to be placed on a par with profit "because laughter and play and fun on the job can help create a culture of caring and connection in the workplace that is just as important—if not more so—than productivity and profitability." (Weinstein 1996, 24).

Energizing Meetings and Conventions

What prompted Mobil Oil to hire the Temptations, Mary Wilson of the Supremes, Martha Reeves and the Vandellas, and the Four Tops to entertain eighty-five hundred of its dealers at a Las Vegas meeting? It wasn't a tough decision. Previous meetings had fallen flat. They were too often dreary, uneventful events that failed to pique much interest or spark any real energy. With this dreary experience behind and another opportunity coming up, Mobil saw a chance to add one plus one plus one and yield ten. The universal appeal of the Motown sound was embellished with spectacular orchestral arrangements written for the Nevada Symphony Orchestra and backed by a seventy-voice black choir supporting the aging icons. For the first time, what was normally received with little joy became a company-sponsored two-and-one-half-hour fun-filled frenzy. Dealers, distributors, and managers, along with the guys who pump gas, danced wildly in their chairs and joined others on tabletops. The musicians were driven to an even higher performance.

To what end were all these hijinks aimed? Through the universal language of music, primitive and familiar, those in attendance let go and played together. This evening built bonds that previous events never touched. It built loyalty toward a company that would invest so lavishly in its people's sheer joy if only for an evening. But it was an evening that created memories that would last a lifetime, embellished and retold as part of the company's legend and lore.

Spoofing and Poking Fun

Funny Business, a Scottsdale, Arizona–based entertainment firm, makes its living by helping organizations to get their message across through humor and scripted stage productions. Dennis Ford, the company's founder, told us in an interview that he believes the quickest way to bring death to an important corporate message at a big meeting is to get some executive behind a podium, dim the lights, and run a slide show—clogged with a hundred bits of information. According to Ford,

> There is no intrinsic value to information; it's what you do with it. . . . If people don't hear the message, they won't remember, and things won't change. We embrace what we feel, we remember things we enjoy not rhetoric.

Whether talking about a new product, a merger, or a cultural message, it is important to begin and end on an upbeat note.

Comedy embraces the creative, the receptive. And there is no more interesting subject than "me." Touch people where they live. If you talk about them, you've got their attention. . . . All in the context of a story, dialogue, and song —that's the formula.

In scripting an event, Ford goes straight for a company's sacred cows and sacrosanct secrets. He gets to these by scribing more than twenty pages of interviews, half with management and the desired message(s); the other half with customers (the audience) and their personal interests. Ford then creates a customized script to get the message across. It can be a Letterman-style show, a newscast, a Donohue piece, a night awards event, or a knockoff of a stage play, musical comedy, or TV show. Whether good news or a wake, it expressly intermingles and weaves the personalities of those in the audience with the facts and foibles of management. Ford says, "Poking fun at themselves humanizes management. People appreciate their stepping outside the box. It's hard to be angry at something you just laughed about."

Funny Business does not rely on laser shows or fancy pyrotechnics. It presents a good story accompanied by powerful music on a decent sound system. Lighting, with a simple pipe and drape backdrop, provides a sparse but sufficient stage setting. The rest is filled in by the imaginations of those in the audience. The largest employer of actors in Arizona, Ford likes using professionals. They are able to let the performance go where needed. Corporate actors are too high risk, often afraid to walk the creative line between truth and fancy. Their use is weighed against the potential reward. Do they like to act? Will they come to five rehearsals? Will they make their character look his or her best? Through theater, Funny Business expresses issues that are hard to communicate or too sensitive to confront. In the "play," a company sees its virtues and vices. Management can deliver messages that few other media could get across as well.

Serious Play

Funny Business does not restrict the use of play to management issues. It ventures into other sensitive territory where play can make a serious point. The issue of diversity is a good example. In many situations, racial, gender, or other differences are treated with kid gloves. People flock to those who are like them. Then they "walk on eggs" around issues that separate them from others.

Tommy George, CEO of Motorola, wanted to communicate boldly to employees that "we are worldwide." After a consulting team was brought in and failed miserably with their wall maps and global trends, Motorola called Funny Business. Ford asked the head of Motorola's diversity program for five behaviors they would most like to change. Then sketches were built that were real and politically (in)correct, such as the following, described to us by Ford:

> A new segment vice president ran out the party line that if you were a thirty-eight-year-old white male, you didn't stand a chance. "With all this diversity crap," he said, "you needed to be a woman named Martinez." People laughed their way through the nervousness of the truth. The lights came up and the segment vice president gave permission for anyone in the audience who had never heard this to leave. Then the message was clear, "Not only are we not gonna' do this anymore, it's wrong. It's just plain wrong."

A parody or spoof allows serious messages to be put out where people can view them less self-consciously. It is a form of play that eases the delivery of the controversial message and gets the desired results.

Play Organizers

Certain stimuli are almost guaranteed to get people into a playful mood. Whether those stimuli are mascots, children, role reversals, or other symbols of play, their presence brings out something special in most people, even those who are typically serious and uptight.

Mascots

Company mascots can have a pervasive, mobilizing effect on a workforce. In recognition of this, mascot schools are springing up around the country. They teach people how to behave dressed as Big Bird, Mickey Mouse, or whatever character a company has adopted as a symbolic focal point. At a midwestern hospital, the official mascot is Huggy Bear, a large, fuzzy pink bear who wanders the hallways twenty-four hours a day giving employees and patients hugs. But mascots can even be inanimate objects, like Bobby Band-Aid and the Band-Aid Band singing "Stuck on You."

A member services representative in a managed health care organization told us the following story:

> Rags the Pup was a stuffed animal that took the punches when customers got testy, which they regularly did, in our member services department. All we ever heard was complaints, and some of our customers got pretty out of line. We had to smile through it, but when we hung up, we called for Rags, and he would sail over the booth walls to get a beating or be talked to rather smartly. Pretty soon, frustration turned into laughter. Everyone should have such a mascot.

Standard, universally recognized icons, such as Santa Claus, the Easter Bunny, and Elvis, can have a similar effect and light up a workplace.

Children

Many companies are creating opportunities to bring family closer to work. "Bring Your Child to Work" days and daycare on the premises put children closer to the workplace. Celebrations involving family usually call for clowns, toys, games, fairs, balloons.

Featuring employees in younger days as children is another well-known motif. Baby pictures of employees, especially executives, are used for entertainment and to introduce a common denominator: We were all young once. Children are natural players and their presence, in one way or another, brings out the best of our childhood, child-like, reminiscences.

Humanizing Leaders or Inverting the Power Structure

Another way to pep up the workplace is to turn the chain of command on its head. Role reversal can humanize whoever is on top and offer a chance for lower-ranking employees to let off a little steam. A new, upside-down hierarchy is established on occasions such as Boxing Day in some parts of Canada, where the workers become bosses for the day. This provides a playful chance for everyone to know how it feels in the other's situation.

Harvey Cox, in his book *Feast of Fools*, shows how festival and fantasy play a less central role among us now than in the days of holy fools, mystical visionaries, and a calendar full of festivals. He recalls the Feast of Fools, which was celebrated in medieval Europe around January 1 with revelry and satire; no custom or convention was spared ridicule. The highest ranking personages were lampooned. It is healthy, he feels, for a culture periodically to make sport of its most sacred practices. Accepted values are inverted, subjects become kings, and foolishness rules the day.

Music

The power of music is well known in commercial settings where Muzak provides the backdrop intended to motivate shoppers to exchange hard-earned dollars for sought-after goods. Tunes are powerful precipitants of feelings, and a march, ditty, or upbeat piece can produce delight and energy. (See chapter 11 for specific music suggestions.)

Productivity can soar or sink with every change in music venue (a musical Hawthorne effect), but classical music is said to sustain the greatest effect over time, producing the highest output on an ongoing basis. Victoria's Secret is an example of a firm that takes full advantage of the power of classical music. The company not only pipes Bach and Mozart into its six-hundred-plus retail outlets but merchandises it directly to customers. The approach has been so successful that Victoria's Secret has now become the largest single retail source of classical music in the country ("Along with Peignoirs, Top-Selling CDs," *New York Times*, 19 January 1997).

Festive Symbols

The presence of balloons, flowers, costumes, desserts, and candles all connote party spirit, universally encouraging people to drop their guard and become playful. As Sister Corita King observes: "Ice a cake, light sparklers, and sing, and something celebrative may happen" (Cox 1996, 108).

Plain and Simple Ways to Play

A number of recent books are devoted to teaching us something we should already know—how to play at work.

★ Bob Nelson's *1001 Ways to Reward Employees*

★ Barbara Glanz's *Care Packages: Dozens of Little Things You Can Do to Regenerate Spirit at Work*

★ Matt Weinstein's *Managing to Have Fun*

★ Leslie Yerkes and Dave Hemsath's *301 Ways to Have Fun at Work*

The problem is that many of us have either temporarily forgotten or misplaced our innate gift—or reserve it for the hours before 9 A.M. or after 5 P.M. These authors promote play as a way to reinvigorate the workplace. They also highlight play's practical results. Even though it's not the real object, it pays to play. Their ideas are shamelessly simple and emerge mainly from the thoughtfulness, resourcefulness, and creativity people generate when they set aside time for frolic and fun. Play need not be lavish to make its mark.

The play spirit can enter any activity. Here is a compendium of plain and simple ways to pump fun into the various types of celebrations, rituals, and ceremonies delineated earlier.

MARKING TIME

- Mark milestones publicly: Post timelines and encourage people to color in their progress.

- Rewrite the corporate history with flip charts and pictures of characters, significant events, key words, and phrases. Create scrapbooks or mock time capsules.

- Find a festive reason to celebrate every month. Invite people to dress or act in accordance with the spirit of the occasion.

- Hold a companywide "It's Our Birthday" party by exchanging names for cards and gifts under $5.

- Do anything on a regular day of the week or month or year— bring your pet, go out to lunch, dress down.

- Give Joy Breaks on a regular basis, inviting people to invent their own form of festivity.

- Choose from hundreds of ways to celebrate people's birthdays, newborns, marriages, graduations, and major life passages.

- Capitalize on companywide anniversary dates by hosting fun events.

RECOGNITION AND ACKNOWLEDGMENT

- Have a "Thank You Circle," where people can recognize others for their contributions.

- Use props (common everyday items) that are symbols of what you wish to recognize. Confer them as awards with a playful ceremony.

- Smile and say thank you when you catch people going out of their way on behalf of employees or customers. Write personal notes and make personal phone calls saying thanks.

- Ask people to create certificates of self-recognition and distribute them for others to confer the award. This can be done with individuals or teams.

- Convene spontaneous gatherings and let people ask for a standing ovation honoring a good deed or a job well done.

- Distribute gold-sealed Star Certificates declaring employee ownership of specific stars in the galaxy, with a star album and star verification records (as IBM, Coca-Cola, Ford, Monsanto, and Nikkon have done).

- Give anonymous gifts recognizing special contributions to enliven the daily drudge.

- Give time off, flextime, sabbaticals.

- Use a photo, with a blurb acknowledging the person in some way. Blow it up into a poster to be displayed in a public place.

- Create opportunities for peers to cheer peers. Have colleagues select worthy candidates and dream up deserving awards and presentations. Practice toasting.

- Pass a symbolic award around— each winner to the next.

RENEWAL RITUALS

- Celebrate your survival of anything. Tell stories on different views of the ups and downs.

- Create a team cheer and chant it at the beginning or ending of a workday or event.

- Do a collective visioning exercise: group members paint their dreams on paper and then work together to build a composite of the entire group.

- Celebrate the mission of the organization through elevation of its symbols—pictures, objects, music, stories of heroes and heroines.

- Wear the company colors and use the company products. Be a customer for a day (public mystery shopper).

- Go on retreat. Use formal and informal time to build team spirit.

- Have a brainstorming session for a company logo or theme.

- Create an oath of office or a swearing-in ceremony.

- Give out company symbols on paraphernalia that people really need and use. Spread the perks around.

- Call on business units to contribute a celebration of the company and its mission.

- Communicate widely and well. Information binds.

- Have dazzling training and development programs.

- Make music, dance, or create art together.

- Incorporate everyone in the creation of acts of renewal.

COMINGS AND GOINGS

- Decorate the office of a new employee. Have an agenda planned for introductions, a map for getting around, and a list of tips from coworkers.

- Create a welcoming ritual promoting the person's unique talents.

- Assign advocates for the initiates, to sponsor their introduction each day for the first two weeks.

- Before a colleague's departure, post a flip-chart easel with an open-ended statement and markers for people to anonymously contribute their thoughts. "I would really like to say this to (Bill): (complete the thought)." Read aloud and then give it ceremoniously to the departing person.

- If appropriate, host a roast of the departing colleague. Give simple gifts, symbols of admiration and accomplishment.

- Bury your past—have a funeral and toss the ideas or undesirable thoughts onto a pyre.

- Have teams select a song that expresses farewell, perform it and videotape it.

- Tell stories of how it was when . . .

- Create a sacred space—a portal, for example—through which all initiates and retirees must pass.

ALTRUISTIC PLAY

- Rally around a cause—a national disaster or a local tragedy.

- Give time off for contributions to worthy causes.

- Give a gift of self as a group, for example, build a house through Habitat for Humanity.

- Commit random acts of kindness.

- Pull families, customers, suppliers, and communities into your celebrations.

- Collect money and goods to distribute to those in need.

- Adopt families or charitable organizations and totally focus on their well-being.

- Plow the wealth of your company into social good. Create a community profit-sharing program.

- Give away what you do well (education, aesthetics, goods and services).

- Become coaches or tutors for those in need.

- Don't forget that there are people in need inside your organization.

- Hire those needing some help procuring jobs—the elderly, prisoners on work release, young people, moms. Work is dignity.

- Remind people of what it is to be kind. Model it.

- Start a "kindness campaign."

PURE PLAY

- Hold a "Thank goodness it's . . . (anything—Friday, not raining, or whatever)."

- Provide food, champagne, treats at any juncture. Order in for a communal lunch.

- Pull together a group and ask them to find something that deserves celebrating—then have them create the celebration on the spot.

- Challenge participants to write raps, songs, poetry, ads, or plays on any theme, and then dramatize them.

- Turn on music and have someone teach some kind of dancing.

- Have a meeting off-site followed by a social event.

- Create any occasion that requires costumes.

- Take pictures of everyday work fun and post them.

- Designate a bulletin board as a place for employees to post favorite jokes, cartoons, communications. Attach these to more mundane memos. Create a humor room. Take a daily humor break or have a laugh-a-day challenge for someone to tell a joke. Publish the jokes.

- Instead of a holiday bonus in a check, give cash; go on a group shopping spree and play show-and-tell upon returning.

- Do anything exchanging the roles of bosses and employees: Prepare meals; wait on employees; clean up; do each others' jobs for a day.

- Organize any kind of contest, lottery, drawing, marathon, or sports event and try to work it so that everyone wins.

We conclude as we began, by drawing on the work of Johan Huizinga.

> Business becomes play. The process goes so far that some of the great business concerns deliberately instill the play spirit into their workers to step up production. The trend is now reversed: play becomes business (p. 200).

Play is an authentic, exuberant activity created to call forth the human spirit. Leaders, as instigators of play, are risk takers, willing to become vulnerable, to go out on a limb, and to create a culture of playfulness—some of it planned, some spontaneous. There is much work ahead to infuse today's workforce with frolic and fun. As Herb Kelleher of Southwest Airlines maintains, "Fun is not a four-letter word, fear is."

PART THREE

Fundamentals of Fun

Chapter 10

Setting the Stage:
The Making of Meaningful Events

> **You cannot learn by copying. First, it assumes that you can figure out what someone else *did*. Secondly, it assumes that if you did the same thing, it would work the same way for you. These are both fallacies.**
>
> —W. Edwards Deming

Copying anything you learn here—or anywhere else—will rarely work. What soars in one company may fall flat in another. Heart-grabbing, soulful events are attuned to cultural values. To succeed, they must be historically rooted, relevant to the contemporary mood, and aimed toward shaping the future. Mimicking someone else's occasion almost always backfires. Our intent is to provide ideas you can adapt to fit your particular context. The examples we present are to be used as "sourdough starter" to get your own creative juices flowing. But there is one iron-clad maxim to be heeded: Intimate knowledge of deeply held cultural patterns and practices is an absolute prerequisite to creating a successful event.

In addition to the one universal maxim mentioned above, there are a few other guiding principles for designing a gripping gathering, which this chapter will begin to articulate. Part of the design challenge is finding your organization's own unique style or signature. Every act of celebration is a work of art—it bears the signature of the organization, its culture, and its designers. The best celebrations are authentic—they come both from the heart and the head. The goal is to assemble a gathering that is fun, engaging, and speaks to the hearts and souls of everyone present.

There are masters of the art of the party, people like Joe Jeff Goldblatt, Renny Reynolds, and Martha Stewart, all of whom have written books on the subject. But we want to extend their teachings to examine the inner workings of corporate rituals and ceremonies, to discover the critical ingredients for putting magic in the moment.

Identifying the Key Ingredients

Setting the stage for successful celebrations requires attention to selecting the right ingredients: choosing a theme, rounding up the right people, arranging the setting, orchestrating the mood, and providing the right accoutrements—the delighters—which means identifying the key symbols, accentuating communication through movement, and encouraging spontaneity and theater.

For many corporate types, all this may loom as an overwhelming task. That is why executives sometimes choose to call on special events planners or celebration specialists, individuals who make planning occasions their business. In the beginning, a good planner will ask questions such as those on the Preplanning Questions on the next page. For Patsy Bruce, owner of Events Unlimited, these questions are a routine part of her preassessment of party clients.

Bruce tells her about-to-be-hosts, "You're there to change history. Think *special!*" as opposed to the type of event she describes in the following story:

> The CEO was giving away money to salesmen who had sold anywhere from $200,000 to $800,000 of his product that year. He was doing this in an armory decorated with crepe paper, with music provided by an old boom box. His secretary planned the event. She did her best and I have to give her credit; it was the best crepe paper party I've ever seen. Now there's nothing wrong

PREPLANNING QUESTIONS

1. Why are you having this event?

2. What do you want to accomplish? What is the message?
   Reward? Bad year but we're okay? We are better than the competition?

3. What is your history of celebrating?

4. Has attendance grown?

5. What did you learn the last time you did this?
   What worked and what didn't?

6. What is the condition of the company?
   Have you had a bad year? Have you had a good year?

7. Where are the people?
   Interview employees.

with a crepe paper party. But you wouldn't send an engraved invitation to a crepe paper party. Therefore you wouldn't invite salesmen who had made you a fortune that year either.

Selecting a Theme

Most meaningful events have a theme. Earlier chapters have provided a framework for choosing an appropriate theme, which we will review.

★ *Seasonal, cyclical occasions and milestones*: The calendar almost always provides a convenient reason for an event that draws people closer to each other and dramatizes key values. Feasts and festivity arise naturally around Thanksgiving, the winter solstice, or the summer picnic, for example.

★ *Recognition and reward*: Another popular theme for expressive events is appreciation and acknowledgment. Gathering to recognize and reward people who exemplify through daily deeds a company's vision and values has both a personal and communal payoff. Individuals receive their time in the spotlight for accolades and applause. Others have an opportunity to cheer and to witness and to relish shared and sacred commitments. The word commemorate combines the words come, remember, and celebrate. The event becomes a showcase of important corporate values.

★ *Triumph and victory*: A third theme highlights collective achievements—launching a new product, celebrating an important milestone, or dedicating a new building. These are the "Hurray, We Made It!" occasions that provide a welcome spiritual uplift and rejuvenation.

★ *Calamity or defeat*: Not everything always works out as originally conceived. Every company has its down times as well as its high points. The "Oops, We Didn't Make It" or "How Could This Have Happened to Us?" happenings provide an opportunity to exalt together in the hope that better times lie ahead.

★ *Entrances and exits*: A fifth theme for ritual and ceremony stems from key personnel transitions—new people arriving, veterans leaving (voluntary or otherwise), promotions, and demotions.

★ *Comfort and letting go*: A sixth type of affair deals with the existential loss associated with mergers, sellouts, or the introduction of new practices that make old practices obsolete. These events mix comfort with joy, providing opportunities for people to acknowledge loss and begin the process of healing.

★ *Altruism*: Yet a seventh theme convenes people in celebration of their collective efforts to help others—the United Way, adopting a family for the holidays, Habitat for Humanity, to name a few.

★ *Pure play*: There is always room for ritual and ceremony convened "just for the hell of it."

For every celebration there is a *raison d'être*—a why—that must be carefully realized and addressed. Crafting effective celebrations means attending to both the prevailing cultural issues and the organization's enduring, unique identity. Whatever is celebrated sends signals about what is valued. This gives the event

---

THEME POINTS

- Organize around a theme.
- Celebrate often, seasonally and sporadically.
- Know the values you wish to exemplify.
- Be authentic.
- Be true to your cultural ways.
- Be sensitive when traditional ways must be changed.

---

designer a symbolic focal point for setting the stage. Having a single theme also helps to coalesce ingredients into a meaningful enterprise.

Rounding up People

Celebrations are about building relationships—bonding. Events also can be a form of internal marketing to build team spirit among individual people. Involving employees in planning is one way to assure the calibration of the event to the audience. Southwest's Culture Committee, the group that oversees the airline's celebrations, includes a cross section of people from functions across the company. The only qualification: they must have big hearts. Not a bad criterion for selecting the right people to plan. In the following story, Patsy Bruce raises awareness of the critical role of party planners in creating an effective celebration.

> In one company, the person who has been in charge of the annual event—as the company grew from being ten people in the sales department to twenty-five hundred dealers—has been the vice president's assistant. She is suddenly in charge of a $9 million party budget and the most important function of the year. I'm constantly astounded at the irony. Of course, it is the most fun the assistant has all year. Since it's the most fun, she guards her territory. And that makes the professional's job much more difficult.

Who Should Be There?

There is nothing inherently wrong with a solitary celebration; we do it all the time to mark personal milestones and special events. But intensity grows in the company of others. We want to be able to say: "The whole world was there, we had the right people, and no one was excluded." The able party planner knows the richness provided by the right mix of people. In *Entertaining*, Martha Stewart recommends guests with both compatible and conflicting interests, to support at least gentle controversy as opposed to silent accord. Well-managed diversity—mixed viewpoints and walks of life—encourages creative tension. Ceremony helps us pull people together, particularly when a situation is pluralistic. Inclusion works miracles in bonding people of different levels, races, sexes, and functions into a united community. NRDC, Nortel's telephone repair division, for example, recently made a change in who attends its annual operations review. According to one employee, "It used to be just the top brass, the managers. Now it's the teams that come. In fact, it's open to everyone. It has become a real event."

Guests in the Right Light

The designers of a truly great occasion view guests as clients or customers. Customers, like everyone else, have a variety of needs that must be thought through, from basic subsistence to higher order. The objective is to address as many needs as possible, leaving the guest feeling honored, special, taken care of, safe. The following story, told to us by a computer technician at a prominent law firm, is an example of what we mean.

> I love where I'm working now. My firm had just signed a huge client. The partners shut down the place at four o'clock one afternoon and rounded us up for a surprise party on the fourth floor. The message was, "You are part of the victory! We did this!" They made us totally comfortable and there were no big dudes—just food, friendliness, alcohol for those who wanted it, nonalcoholic beverages for those who didn't. You know, they even had someone to drive you home if you needed it. This is the kind of place I've been looking for.

The next story is the antithesis of what we are talking about.

> It was the annual graduation ceremony. Hundreds of parents, friends, and relatives gathered on the campus to see their loved ones honored. As this was a prestigious university, the audience was full of future well-heeled givers of significant sums. Most were seated in the ninety-eight-degree sun in folding lawn chairs. The music was canned. The flowers were wilted. The dean gave a nearly one-hour speech on world poverty—a subject far afield from the minds of the celebrants on this day. Then a lower-level functionary gave out the diplomas.

This example shows almost total blindness to the guests. To avoid such miscalculations, a buy-in process might be worth the effort.

The Buy-In

You may have seen a celebration work elsewhere, but what effect will it have on your crowd? Many leaders will make a command decision themselves about what a celebration should be or delegate it with total discretion to a department—for example, human resources or public relations. A more consultative way is to have a representative group of customers—a committee or focus group—examine and react to a tentative plan.

We were told the following story by a hospital executive, a nun, about how she learned the simple art of the pilot test.

> I once said to a consultant, "I don't know what reaction my memos get. I send out these one-way communications to the masses, and I never hear back. What impact did they have on the receiver?" The consultant suggested I pilot test the communication with a small representative group of participants, asking them for feedback and honest reactions. This has now become one of my tried and true strategies.

Another hospital administrator had a public relations firm develop a video to be shown at the annual leadership retreat. Taking advice from an outside consultant, he previewed it with a representative group of employees. Their reaction was: "It's the stupidest thing we've ever seen. We hope you didn't have to pay anything for it." Needless to say, the video was not shown at the event.

Getting reactions is important, but better yet, ask an interested crew to create the celebration, a la the Culture Committee of Southwest Airlines.

Begin in the Beginning

The manner in which people are invited carries one of two messages, either "You are special" or "You are an insignificant part of the cattle call." Is the invitation personalized, artistic, signed, calligraphied? How much original thought went into its appeal to the participants?

Following are some noteworthy options:

★ A brass theater ticket invitation on a key chain

★ A 3-D pop-up of the building being commemorated

★ Audiotapes or a CD announcement

★ A roll-out scroll tied with a ribbon

★ A magnetized card

★ A brass mask mounted on marble

Appropriate Dress Code

A major component of comfort is specified by an appropriate dress code. Some people are happy in formal attire while others only feel at home in casual dress. Defining the limits and having guidelines that embrace attendees' ideas are important. If their idea of dressed up is a hillbilly tuxedo, then a black-tie requirement is going to bomb. Patsy Bruce, professional event planner, gives the following advice:

> I cannot imagine that the line workers in a plant would want to go to a black-tie dinner at the botanical gardens. However, they do want to get dressed up for the Christmas party. Put them in an environment where they can get dressed up and be comfortable, whatever their dressed up is. Whatever his tuxedo is, make him happy he came in it.

Why, in 1996, were more adults than children dressed up for Halloween or taking in Disneyworld? An October 30, 1996, USA *Today* cover story headlined, "Workers' Halloween Exodus Growing," offers an explanation.

> More companies are finding that parents are taking time off to "supervise" their children's trick-or-treating (undoubtedly they want to accompany their children and relive some of the past). To curb the Halloween brain drain, more companies are moving celebration into the workplace. Sentry, a safe maker in Rochester, New York, has scheduled two parties—with costume parade and haunted house—to accommodate all three shifts.

Adults want their turn at costumes, fantasy, and play. Some people enjoy wearing costumes on holidays or having contests like ugly shoe/ugly tie day, or Ben & Jerry's clash dressing day. "Casual Day" is another corporate way of costuming. There are other ideas, too, such as dress like your favorite holiday destination or dress like your clients, that can put an amusing spin on a fun event.

Names and Identity

The first necessity in making people feel special is recognizing them by name. To be addressed and included means others know who you are. Attention to simple details assures a sense of identity. This is conveyed in advance by personalized invitations. At the event, names can be broadcast on name tags or placards, which must be easy to read in order to prevent awkward moments of forgetting someone's name. Nothing makes attendees feel more uncomfortable than forgetting momentarily the name of someone

---

PEOPLE POINTS

- Build relationships.
- Be as inclusive as possible, as long as it promotes comfort.
- Invitations speak in many ways—choose the right message.
- Encourage diversity along with compatibility.
- Honor guests. Treat them as customers.
- Appreciate the clothing preferences of your guests.
- Respect the importance of names. Make sure guests are known through some method of introduction.

they should know. Similarly, there is very little that can make people feel more unspecial than a boss or colleague not remembering their names.

Current U.S. Postmaster General Marvin Runyon, during his leadership of both Nissan and the Tennessee Valley Authority, insisted that name tags be worn on a person's right side rather than the left to make reading the name a more natural part of a ritual greeting. If the event is primarily seated, a preplanned seating chart and assigned table facilitators encourage interaction and strategic mixing of participants. Formal introductions also elevate the person by name and affiliation.

Arranging the Setting

People's comfort extends beyond names and faces to include the actual spot where an event is held. A special environment transforms human experience into a compelling occasion and transports people to a spirit-infused place. Although the workplace is always a potential setting for celebration, there is usually magic in physically "getting away," in psychologically carrying people to a new venue. To the extent that nature, beauty, light, and open space are incorporated, people are themselves inspired. Aesthetics make us feel uplifted, ennobled and tap the well of the human spirit. What is conveyed by the environment reaches participants. Once again, Patsy Bruce has some advice.

> Put them in an environment. The other important, never-break rule is to put people in an environment where they have permission to have fun. And create that permission—by the way the room feels, by the way the room looks, by the way the room sounds, by the whole thing.

Standard party settings are hotel ballrooms, people's homes, and restaurants, but think creatively. Why not a barn or a theater stage or a sheep pasture or the bed of a trailer truck?

Several years ago, the administrators of the Beaverton School District in Oregon met at the superintendent's office for their annual summer retreat. There was more than the usual grousing because the group was used to going somewhere special for the meeting. Dr. Jim Hagar, the superintendent, welcomed everyone and then announced that the group would be boarding buses for a journey to a yet-to-be-determined destination. The group filed out and boarded yellow school buses for a magical trek through time. After an hour's trip, they arrived at an old winery located in a beautiful Oregon vineyard.

As the administrators filed off the buses, they spotted tables topped with placards in front of the main entrance. Each listed a decade: the 1940s, 1950s, 1960s, and so forth. Administrators were asked to sit at a table that would include the year they first joined the district. Scribes, assigned to each table prior to the event, were asked to bring along old annuals, newspapers, and artifacts from each decade's ten-year reign. At the respective tables, groups were asked to come up with a skit, a poem, or a song representing their era.

> **SETTING POINTS**
> - Mentally and physically transport the participants.
> - Create an atmosphere of beauty, safety, freedom, grace, respect.
> - Stress openness, flexibility, and informality.
> - Scale the setting to the customers.

As the sun set behind the winery, the presentations unfolded. All were both poignant and hilarious. The last group to present was composed of the year's new hires. Their presentations capped off the evening and the entire assembly adjourned for a wine tasting.

Comfort is a primary concern for all of us. We enter a domain scanning for signs of danger and assessing where we will fit comfortably. Witness restaurant patrons' behavior of lining the walls first, in order to have a clear view of the exit. Notice people at cocktail parties eyeing the door. Lowered lighting—in between dim and harsh—provides more safety than bright exposure. Small groupings of six to eight put people at ease in large group settings.

Orchestrating the Mood

There is an intangible quality to any gathering that could be characterized as the "mood" or the "energy." Mood is orchestrated—partially synergistic, mostly ephemeral. All of the aforementioned ingredients—setting, design, costumes, players—come together and something (or nothing) happens. Call it chemistry.

Each type of celebration has its desired tone. Symbols, decor, music, costumes, and language are chosen to support the desired feel. The pace feels like the correct rhythm. Contrast a spirited revival with a somber, reverent farewell to the bygone, or with the elaborate Arabian Nights ball in honor of an eighteen-year-old San Francisco debutante described by Jody Shields in the November 1996 *Vanity Fair.*

> Open sesame they did. A painted backdrop of the Amber Palace in Jaipur blanketed the building's facade. Costumed genies carrying beaded maharajah umbrellas escorted guests up a carpeted entryway lined with Duquette's [an-82-year-old Los Angeles designer] signature coral painted trees. Twelve thousand square feet of quilted hangings stitched by a tent wallah in Delhi were draped throughout the courtyard. Orchids and wildflowers overflowed from gilded bird-cages. Carved idols crouched on every table and any available floor space. Peter Duchin and his orchestra were enshrined in an elaborate pavilion. As for costumes, all the generations shared the fantasy. Ladies of all ages glittered, showed off bosoms and tummies—but no pierced navels here.

Snake charmers, a whirling dervish, and the Peter Duchin orchestra entertained six hundred guests in what one observer described as "a perfectly theatrical experience." Although exceptional and high budget, this celebration presents a vivid example of the majestic, magical side of life. Forget the costs, savor the moment, and enjoy the memories for a lifetime. No one ever forgets such dramatic high points. Everything changes—lighting, music, words, feelings expressed. The tone is set by the leaders, the participants, and the design itself. People take their cue and act accordingly. And then reenact the event later in their minds and in their stories.

MOOD POINTS

- Calibrate mood to the theme.
- Design for it.
- Stand back and let it happen.

Who would know better than an evangelist minister the chemistry of ceremony and celebration? Kate McVeigh, a guest minister who also has her own radio show, commented to us:

Every time we come together it is a celebration. . . . We rejoice because of our personal relationship with God—it comes from within. We have joy whether we have had a good day or a bad day. Life is a celebration and we have gratitude for everything God has done for us.

I open a service with a prayer (a pause), to ask God to open our eyes, to speak to us. I close the same way, with prayer, to encourage action from what they know. There are praise services, with upbeat music, and there are worship services, with slower songs, like Thanksgiving.

Hymnals, they bring their own Bibles, pianos, drums—we use any instrument. I tell stories, personal stories, and use lots of humor; it helps to open the door. There can be a pulpit, sometimes flowers. If it's a small audience, I walk among them, ask questions.

There are powerful words, such as "thank you."

The Good News is that

You are loved.

You have a special place.

You have the free gift of salvation.

God is a good God, who loves every person and has a plan for their life.

Celebrate. Enjoy the Good News and the life God has given you.

McVeigh's approach contains so many of the ingredients of an effective gathering: opening and closing rituals, appropriate music, stories, humor, flowers. Although hers is a religious event, the principles she follows are just as applicable to any ecumenical or secular gathering. Celebration requires feeling in festivity. Call it *soul*. In *Feast of Fools*, Harvey Cox describes festivity as a socially approved occasion for the expression of feelings that are normally repressed or neglected. Festivals, ritual, and ceremony of all kinds summon the human spirit and spawn memories that last a lifetime.

Planning Is Essential

Creating the context for celebration cannot be left to chance; planning is essential. Many of the principles discussed by Max DePree in *Leadership Is an Art*, and used by him to build a quality work environment, also apply to the construction of celebration environments. He advises us to set a stage that accomplishes the following:

★ encourages an open community and fortuitous encounter,

★ welcomes all,

★ changes with grace,

★ is person-scaled,

★ is subservient to human activity,

★ enables the community to reach continually toward its potential,

★ is a contribution to the landscape as an aesthetic and human value,

★ meets the needs we can perceive,

★ is open to surprise,

★ is open to conflict,

★ is nonprecious and nonmonumental (p. 126).

The needs of your audience (customers) for comfort and safety, genuineness, inclusiveness, and identity are all aspects to be consciously crafted and spiritually attuned in advance. Then the conveners must let go, stand back, and let the celebration create itself.

Chapter 11

Orchestrating the Event

irst-rate celebrations are emotional and full of rapture, appealing to more than just cerebral needs. Artful use of sensory stimuli—sights, sounds, smells, tastes, touch—is accomplished through entertainment (people), decoration, food, and drink.

> **Parties are productions, not unlike theatrical productions. Some have lavish sets and big casts, like Broadway. Others use makeshift spaces and exotic decor. Each has a style, a season, and a *raison d'être*.**
>
> —Martha Stewart

Designers of celebrations are artists, weaving people, setting, and activities into an appealing, buoyant mosaic to evoke heartrending response. People respond to celebratory environments in many ways—physically, mentally, emotionally, spiritually. Musical sounds, attractive smells, appealing food, and special lighting signal comfort, informality, and specialness. Aesthetics, art, and decor feed the full range of our faculties.

Events as Theater

Setting the stage through preplanning assures the right ingredients will be assembled. A second step, orchestration, focuses on how the event will actually unfold. Orchestration begins with anticipating the flow, thinking through the management of time and movement—When is a good time to pause for conversation? Is the presentation too long? The designer of a celebration needs to know the audience and envision the players' needs in relation to the flow of the event. This includes being prepared to speed up, slow down, or pause to incorporate a spontaneous situation while the occasion is underway. A masterful flow draws participants into harmony, captivates them, and transports the entire gathering to a magical, spirit-filled place. The production of a celebration is an act of theatrical balance.

> **THEATER POINTS**
> - Realize that life is a stage and we are part of the cast of characters.
> - All theatrical preparation—scripting, rehearsal, and staging—applies to celebrations.
> - Look beyond the front-stage casting to the backstage credits—director, set designer, lighting, props, costumes—for the work to be done.

Some organizations celebrate all the time—entertainment is their "work." Disney has made celebration a booming business. Both lingo and attitude at Disney are scripted in theatrical parlance. For example, at Disney, as explained in *Built to Last* by James Collins and Jerry Porras,

> Employees are "cast members."
>
> A crowd is an "audience."
>
> A work shift is a "performance."
>
> A job is a "part."
>
> A job description is a "script."
>
> A uniform is a "costume."
>
> The personnel department is "casting."
>
> Being on duty is being "onstage."
>
> Being off duty is being "backstage" (p. 128).

In their training program manual, *The Disney Approach to Quality Service*, Disney trainers describe their approach to casting. The show is everything at Disney, and anyone who deals directly with Disney's guests—its visitors—is a host or hostess. New hires learn appropriate behaviors in "showmanship." The guidelines for guest service are as follows:

★   Make eye contact and smile.

★   Greet and welcome each and every guest.

★   Seek out guest contact.

★   Resolve a service failure before it becomes a problem.

★   Display appropriate body language at all times.

★   Preserve the "magical" guest experience.

★   Thank each and every guest (pp. 3–12 and 3–13).

Disney's success formula is built on the following thoughtful premise:

> A quality cast experience generates a quality guest experience—
> if supported by high-quality business practices.

Business Theater

In the world outside of Disney, an alternative term is coming into use for meetings: *business theater*. Mark Thomson, a producer for hire, defines business theater as any meeting or event that needs more than a flat, slide-show presentation. Business theater involves fireworks, mood lighting, magic, singing, storytelling, and dancing.

For example, when Mark was hired to orchestrate the World Food Prize ceremony in the spring of 1996, one thing he did to jazz up a ceremony that has always had a dry academic tone was to hire John Denver to perform. But that's not all. He also assembled child singers from Des Moines–area schools, designed the production, which was staged at the Civic Center, and helped script the event to quicken its pace.

As reported by Mark Couch in the May 4, 1997, *Sunday Tennessean*,

> "He [Thomson] gave the event a balance of substance with a touch of warmth and, I'll use the word, entertainment," said Herman Klipper, World Food Prize executive director. "He had the show down to the minute and told us it's too long there. He helped us remember that we had an audience and they're not all academics."

Designing the Production

Celebration is drama, and planners of celebration must take all the production aspects into account in drawing up the design. According to the Freibergs,

> Southwest Airlines uses three roles to design an event:
>
> > The imagineer, who can envision the impact of an event on participants.
> >
> > The artist, who takes the concept to reality through elements like song, story, balloons.
> >
> > The evoker or the catalyst, who draws people into a spirit of celebration and invites them to initiate their own celebrations (Freiberg and Freiberg 1996, 198–199).

Pace

Pacing or tempo is the rate at which the events unfold, the heartbeat or pulse of the script. In *Special Events: The Art and Science of Celebration*, Joe Jeff Goldblatt says,

> Tempo requires that the special events planner become a perceptive forecaster and, like a maestro, be able to speed up or slow down the tempo where required (p. 37).

Any good score leaves ample room for interpretation, keeping in mind the needs of the guests. Do they want to network and meet people or reflect in quiet observance? Mood can be upbeat, punctuated by laughter and frivolity; or toned down, as in quiet observance of a noble act or a lost friend.

A wedding ceremony provides a good example of changes in tempo: As the ceremony begins, guests may be seated, quietly absorbing melodic tunes such as "Jesu, Joy of Man's Desiring." Then comes the majestic "Lohengrin's Wedding Chorus" by Richard Wagner. The bride makes her grand entrance escorted by her entourage, and all stand in honor. Solemn vows are exchanged; ceremonial rituals are performed. Then comes the high-spirited exit, rapid and upbeat—to Mendelssohn's "Wedding March" from A *Midsummer Night's Dream*.

> **DESIGN POINTS**
> - Map the flow of participants through the event.
> - Pay special attention to greetings and partings.
> - Adjust tempo according to the desired result.
> - Captivate all senses.
> - Provide structure, while leaving room for spontaneity.

Tempo is a major contributor to mood, and music is a major mood inducer.

Greetings

Entrances are critical. This is the awkward moment when guests arrive, typically feeling tentative and insecure. The universal greeting of joy is a smile. It also serves, as it does in the animal kingdom, to appease potential foes—"I come in peace." In many cultures, a bow or expression of submission and honoring is used. Consider the Buddhist greeting, "Namaste," which means "I salute the divine in you that is the divine in me."

Following is a description of the opening of an event at Washington and Lee University in Virginia, as described to us by James Whitehead, treasurer emeritus of that institution:

> It was the opening of the university's Lenfest Center for the Performing Arts. The dress was black tie and the opening promised a wonderful evening of dining and entertainment. As the guests arrived, they paraded between two rows of Glee Club members, took champagne from extended trays, and were serenaded all the way to their places. To preserve the memory, at their place setting was a prerecorded cassette of the music they had just heard.

Being acknowledged by an authentic, heart-felt greeting of warmth is disarming and puts participants at ease. A greeter, an escort, or a receiving line is important to get things off on the right foot. In *Special Events* by Joe Goldblatt, Harriette Rose Katz of Gourmet Advisory Services, Inc., advises: "Use your budget to enhance the beginning and the end, as this is what the guest will most remember."

Shaping the Flow

Physical movement lessens anxiety, which is the value of using greeters to facilitate entrance to a party or hired dancers to pull the shy onto the dance floor. Moving guests around, such as giving a tour or giving them a role in the activities, disinhibits them and draws them into the occasion.

Using a process flow map, envision yourself as a guest and anticipate your journey through the event. Think through the flow and what barriers—anticipated or otherwise—might interrupt smooth progression.

In figure 4, the celebration planner envisioned valet parking upon arrival of the guests, then immediate greeting and identification (name tags). Freed of coats and parcels, guests are offered food and drink, but free to choose where to

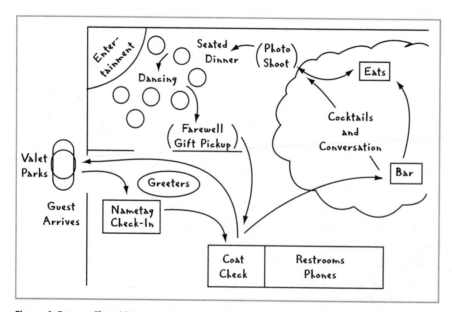

Figure 4. Process Flow Map

move next. The optional photo shot is there for the asking. Dinner is formally seated, with entertainment to come and later the option of dancing. Exit is at the guests' discretion, complete with a farewell and a gift or memento. A simple diagram such as this helps to smooth out the performance in advance.

Beyond Bread: Food Binds

Anthropologists have long known that food carries meaning, mostly as a symbol of union. When people break bread, they come together on a common plane.

Messages can be about inclusion, exclusion, hierarchy, boundaries, transactions. In Mary Douglas's fascinating analysis of a meal, "Deciphering a Meal," she tells us that full meals are for family, close friends, honored guests, while drinks are for strangers, acquaintances, or workmen. The cold meal and barbecue are somewhere in between intimacy and distance. A snack is an unstructured food event, carrying few rules with its consumption.

> **FOOD POINTS**
> - Use food ceremoniously to symbolize union and bountifulness—the best you can afford without overstatement.
> - The type of fare offered conveys your view of participants and the occasion.
> - Food is a core method of communion—don't leave it out or leave it to chance.

Food secures relationships; its giving expresses tenderness, unites groups, and serves as an appeasement gesture to potential enemies (Eibl-Eibesfeldt 1970). Food is offered in religious ceremonies, perhaps to appease angry gods? After all, food is a sedative. A bountiful table is a symbol of wealth.

Food contributes to ceremoniousness in many ways—its volume, order of presentation, difficulty of procurement and preparation, economy or extravagance, degree of seasoning. In our culture, ice cream and cake, champagne, pig roasts, and the like connote celebration.

At a recent gathering of school principals in Washington State, the attendees assembled for the opening dinner. Expecting camp-like food, they were surprised to find several "stations" featuring gourmet food—sushi, prime rib, pasta, sandwiches, hot appetizers, and gorgeous pastries. Beer, wine, and soft drinks were available at several locations. The crowd "grazed" around the food, mingled, and began to bond. The main subject of conversation was the food. It became the universal icebreaker. The food was extraordinary, made everyone feel special, and launched the week's festivities in spectacular style.

Symbols Speak

Symbols are not only words and acts, but are often codified in objects—talismans, charms, amulets. These are physical signs of relationships with people, places, and experiences; of connection and reconnection, union and reunion; of what is sacred to us. (Fulghum 1995). Emotions are touched as the bride descends the aisle, as the nation's flag is unfurled, or as a family gathers at a casket to bid a loved one good-bye. There are some universal symbols, but their meaning also varies from place to place, from person to person, as is shown by the following story told to us by a friend.

> Many people cannot pass a military cemetery without being moved to tears. As my husband and I passed one the other day, we both teared up. I said, "Oh, the nobility of giving your life for your country." "No," he replied, "the waste of human youth."

It is important to clarify meaning before proceeding. Reading the situation through the eyes of various individuals or subcultures beforehand can help prevent a cacophonous event with a lingering bitter aftertaste.

One important symbol is the company logo, and many companies make a point of displaying it handsomely at events. After all, the company is giving the party. Matt Weinstein, CEO of Playfair, believes that appreciation should always be expressed for a team in a public ceremony. He gave out sunglasses with his company's logo on them at a company retreat while everyone was standing in a circle, eyes closed, chanting, "The future's so bright, we're gonna need shades." The chant crescendoed and reappeared several times during the retreat. At another company, Annie, the bookkeeper, was given a "pink slip" from Victoria's Secret as a going-away gift.

> **Ritual protects and heals, ritual symbolizes to all who come to your table seeking rest and renewal that they are enclosed within a sacred space**
>
> —Sarah Ban Breathnach

Gifts and mementos are symbols, and they play on the principle of reciprocity (the recipient owes the giver). The importance of rank is often apparent in gift-giving: crystal and silver to the board, turkeys to the staff. If I give you more, you owe me more. To avoid this reciprocal bind, as well as to discourage excess and encourage thought, some companies are moving to one dollar gifts or donations to charity.

As mentioned before, food has symbolic value. Lavish or lean makes a statement. Champagne, caviar, and beef Wellington tip the scales on extravagant. According to Ginger Kramer, corporate caterer, "When somebody wants prawns, that means they've got money to spend."

Traditions Are Sacred

> **SYMBOL POINTS**
> - Much of culture is codified in symbols.
> - All symbols do not mean the same thing to all people—examine or build common meaning.
> - Use simple, meaningful symbols and confer them with passion.
> - Give gifts with authenticity.
> - Add symbols and props that honor the recipient.

People anticipating a cultural event are typically ambivalent. They want something different, something really spectacular that takes their breath away. On the other hand, they want tradition to prevail. There are some things that happen every year, and people come to expect them. Knowing what to repeat is as important as inventing something new, as is evident from this story told to us by a hospital executive.

> It was hard to fathom. After the holidays, morale bottomed out. Nurses, physicians, staff—everyone acted disgruntled and demoralized. I couldn't figure out why. Finally I called in Sarah, the volunteer coordinator. Everyone talks to her. She's the keeper of the flame. I asked her what was going on. She responded, "What was different about this year's holiday gala?" I thought for a moment before responding: "Sarah, you know times are tough. We just couldn't afford the open bar and the big slice of prime rib this year."
>
> "There's your problem," she said.
>
> "But why?" I asked.
>
> "Are you religious?"
>
> "Yes, why?"
>
> "What faith?"

"Catholic."

"How would you react if they substituted a Cheeze-It cracker and Pepsi in your communion service?"

"You mean . . .?"

"That open bar was a once-a-year chance for toasts and connections. The prime rib symbolized how much the hospital cares for its employees."

"Oh my God!"

"It gets worse. You substituted turkey for the prime rib. Now you've become the turkey to our employees, the Grinch that ruined their holiday event."

Icons Generate Unity

In political, ethnic, and religious groupings, we see formerly diverse and autonomous groups brought together by common ideas, common representatives (heads of state, church figures), and simple emblems. Common symbols make groups out of subgroups. There may be badges, forms of dress, uniforms, or flags. New nations and political groups quickly build memorials, post pictures of their presidents, and display their insignia everywhere (Eibl-Eibesfeldt 1970, 451). Many celebratory companies across the world—Mary Kay Cosmetics, Southwest Airlines, Nordstrom Department Stores—create a floor-to-ceiling family album on their walls, with photos, mementos, gifts, trinkets, articles, and letters. In Florida, Sarasota Memorial Hospital's lobby houses a museum of the hospital's history, as does Halifax Community Health System in Daytona, Florida, and Bryan Memorial Hospital in Lincoln, Nebraska.

Heads of organizations often assume symbolic value. Mary Kay Ash of Mary Kay Cosmetics is herself a symbol to her constituents. Though now disabled by a stroke and unable to speak easily, she lives on as the company's fairy godmother and high priestess, her company having created more female millionaires than any other company in history. Her leadership is conveyed through stories, metaphors, and symbols—for example, the pink Cadillac and diamonds.

Symbols need not be elaborate, but they do need to hold common meaning. A consultant and team member of the Center for Continuous Improvement at Quorum Health Resources, Inc., tells this story about symbolism at a coworker's farewell party.

> It was Margaret's farewell party. About eight of us from the office gathered at my house, and after dinner came the awkward silence of how to say good-bye. Suddenly, our leader stood and held up a vertebra of a large animal, decorated with gold ribbons. "We are conferring upon you the Buffalo Backbone Award to symbolize (for Margaret) what you have learned from your mentor (me)—who wrestled a waiter and the maitre d' until they were convinced we had paid enough at that Vail restaurant to earn the plate decorations (buffalo spine segments) several times over. From this point forth, Margaret, should anyone give you grief, you are to hold up your vertebra and show them what spine you have and the stuff you have learned from us." I was also conferred a bone—and both trophies live proudly displayed by us to this day.

Common everyday items can become icons to be conferred with stirring ceremony. Shared meaning for an otherwise neutral object is a way of building culture—it becomes a secret code connoting "our special knowledge." Facilitators ("Tators") at Logansport Memorial Hospital used potatoes at their graduation ceremony—new potatoes for the grads came from old 'tators with sprouting eyes. At Vanderbilt's Peabody College, a yearly "crystal apple ceremony" provides the school's benefactors an opportunity to bestow a cherished educational symbol on an exemplary teacher from their past. What matters is that the recipient is vested with and honored by the meaning, and that the conferer speaks the reason from his or her heart.

The Role of Communication

Communication, according to Max DePree in *Leadership Is an Art*, performs two important functions—to educate and to liberate. The word *educate* literally means "to lead or draw out"—not to pour in, as has too often been the model in public education. What good communication can draw out is an awareness of the ultimate meaning of working together. If it is true, as Margaret Wheatley says in *Leadership and the New Science*, that information and relationships are the essence of an organization, and if it is true that celebration adds the glue of spirit to an organization, then the question becomes: How do we communicate in a celebratory manner?

What we know about communication is that at least 85 to 93 percent of it is nonverbal. Verbal communication has a very low hit rate; the listener rarely hears exactly what the speaker intends. The most successful communication utilizes two-way interplay, invokes multiple channels (print, verbal, audiovisual), capitalizes on the informal networks of the organization for delivery of the message, is looped and repeated, and is delivered by communication champions—people who feel passionate about the subject. According to Anita Roddick in *Body and Soul*,

> How we [The Body Shop] communicate is gob-smacking. We use every available medium to preach, inspire, and stimulate, and in everything we do—whether it's a simple leaflet or a full-length video—our single-minded passion shines through (p. 145).

Open and passionate communication builds trust, reduces fear, and awakens the heart. Language that emphasizes "we" creates unity. Use of nicknames and code words reinforces cultural membership. Flexibility and inquisitiveness foster a learning organization that openly exchanges ideas.

Testimony

Many celebrations are crowned with a speech given by a leader or invited dignitary or guest. In fact, a search of 1,254 holdings of the Vanderbilt University Library system containing the word *celebration* pulled up predominantly orations, addresses, remarks, historical discourses, essays (read), chronologies, speeches, and sermons. So often, these fail to be inspiring or even meaningful.

The wise speaker speaks to the listening needs of the audience, a sign of having studied the customer intensely. According to David Whyte in *The Heart Aroused*:

> The voice carries the emotional body of the person speaking . . .
> it tells us who is speaking, and, in the meeting room, who has
> come to work (pp. 124–25).

Inspirational Speaking

Inspirational speakers provide an important capstone to celebrations. Sometimes a speaker is selected from within the company; more often, hired from outside. Whichever it is, the speaker's job is to inspire those in attendance. Toastmasters International, the world's largest voluntary training organization, has taught the qualities of inspirational speaking for decades. To be inspirational, you must show an audience that collective self-interest coincides with noble motives.

True inspirational speech grows from within the person. It is highly demanding; it calls for dignity, excellence in style, and an emotional rapport with the audience. An inspirational speaker is putting into words shared aspirations, feelings, and beliefs, not earthshaking new ideas. Use of "we" and "us" is inclusive. Good speeches contain picture words and metaphoric expressions that captivate the imagination and breathe life into the talk. "[T]he inspirational speech meets the audience where they are, expresses their mood and feelings in stirring words, and moves them to a higher plane." (Toastmasters International 1984, 49). While expressing the audience's feelings, more noble emotions can be substituted for selfish ones—for example, hope in place of loss. The delivery must be appropriate to the mood of the occasion, full of stories and illustrations, and aimed for the heart, not the head.

HOW TO GIVE AN INSPIRATIONAL SPEECH

- Express the general feelings of the audience.

- Uplift and attribute further meaning to the feelings of the audience.

- In content, style, and delivery, speak to the listeners' expectations for the occasion.

- Use voice level, modulation, and word pictures to dramatize and raise emotions to a higher plane than in other kinds of speeches.

- Use pause.

—Adapted from Toastmasters International

The word *inspire* literally means "to breathe life into." Many scholars of communication, particularly those interested in creating shared visions, have studied Martin Luther King, Jr.'s "I Have a Dream" speech. In that speech, the careful crafting of language produces a binding image that breathes life into (inspires) its audience. The artistry of the speech is contained in its word pictures—painted images of a free America—and in its delivery—spoken with a personal conviction and a cadence that is musical and mighty. Playing repeatedly on themes of freedom, ancestry, and religion, the crescendo of "I" turns to "We" in mid-speech. It is positive and futuristic; it holds out a vision, but also tells the truth about now; it dramatizes the issues. As Martin Luther King, Jr., gave the speech in 1963, it was stirring, sensual, and dramatic—against the backdrop of Abraham Lincoln's statue.

In its publication, *Advanced Communication and Leadership Program: Specialty Speeches*, Toastmasters International says,

---

SPEECH POINTS

- Communicate with passion.

- Use multiple channels, formal and informal.

- Choose language that reinforces the culture.

- Make it two-way interaction, where possible.

- Tune all nonverbal communication to fit the verbal message.

- Use theater and humor—this is show business.

> The speech to inspire expresses the audience's beliefs, values, and sentiments in a language and style fitting to their shared emotion. It carries with it a kind of truth and courage that inspires others to change emotionally, if only for a short time (p. 7).

Cheerleading

It can be difficult for leaders to convey inspirational messages to their troops in a speech. If that is the case, why not use the mechanisms of cheerleaders for marshaling the energies of a crowd? Cheers, chants, humming, singing in unison, all are tools that can supplement or supplant an inspirational talk, and all cultures bring voice to the occasion through these tools. As Angeles Arrien says in *The Four-Fold Way*:

> Working with the voice in any way, whether it be singing,
> chanting, sounding, or voice induction work, feeds the essence
> of who we are (p. 86).

The Power of Silence

In addition to the prowess of words is the power of silence. Periods of enforced quiet tap the human resources within and permit listening—the vessel of learning. Religious services and civic meetings are often opened with a prayer, a pause to quiet stirring and open a person to spiritual messages; they are often closed in the same way.

The Place of Music

Music is our universal language. Everything in life moves in rhythm—particles, heart rate, respiration. Rhythmic *entrainment*, or the process by which rhythms fall into synchronization, is one of the great organizing principles of the universe, according to Stephan Rechtschaffen, M.D. Pendulum clocks set together in a room will eventually come into sync with one another. Physiological rhythms can be brought into phase with a metronome, even in animals, according to Irenäus Eibl-Eibesfeldt.

John Philip Sousa was aware of this phenomenon in setting his marches at 110 beats per minute (bpm), arousing the breathing and thus the heart. One hundred bpm is a march cadence and 120, disco. The lullaby—touching, charming, soothing, gliding—may be the most uniform musical expression in the world. When listening to lullabies, breathing becomes shallow and regular, as the breather adjusts to the rhythm of a sleeping person. Inhale—rise of the melody; exhale—fall of the melody. Jazz, presented under the same conditions, produces excitement, irregular breathing, and irregular changes in galvanic skin response. The highs and lows mimic vocal language, for example, the upper range for cries, the lower for power. Volume can resemble harsh or soft conversation (Eibl-Eibesfeldt 1970).

Music has tremendous power to stir emotions. In "Songs That Lift Your Spirits," Kathy Passero attributes more power to the melody than to the lyrics or to memory; our bodies get synchronized to the beat so that the music puts us in a low-level trance. Sad songs say so much. Old time rock and roll soothes your soul. Jigs, reels, and peppy tunes suggest dancing or laughter. Passero recommends a list of sure-fire spirit lifters like "I Will Survive" by Gloria Gaynor or

"Respect" by Aretha Franklin. For spirit, try a marching band, an old-time gospel choir, or a parade. In the characteristic style of preaching, praise for the Lord is accompanied by upbeat music; worship and thanksgiving by slower songs. Music can be live—a string quartet, a rock band, a choir, or strolling guitarists—or a rented jukebox or hired disc jockey. The guests can be included in the performance or simply entertained.

Patsy Bruce of Events Unlimited says, "I've found that there are two things that always work if it's a certain kind of celebration: a marching band and an old-time gospel choir."

The most popular songs chosen by corporations are listed in table 3.

The artful placement of music during an event can serve to create or dissolve the tensions of the moment. Composers know this well and can encode such cues unobtrusively. For example, Andrew Lloyd Webber's *Sunset Boulevard* utilizes mixed time signatures (5/8 and 7/8) to create tension in his script; the asymmetry keeps the audience "out of sync" with customary 4/4 pop music. In talking about John Cage, Harvey Cox observed that this avant-garde composer of music believed that all sounds—doorbells, car engines—have an enchantment when we really learn to hear them and that the composer must be a frame for the soul.

1.	New Attitude	16.	One Moment in Time
2.	All Fired Up	17.	I Heard It through the Grapevine
3.	The Best	18.	You Got It
4.	Celebration	19.	Wind Beneath My Wings
5.	I'm So Excited	20.	40 Hour Week
6.	The Power of Love	21.	Don't Worry Be Happy
7.	Ghostbusters	22.	We Are Family
8.	Winners	23.	Nine to Five
9.	Victory	24.	Flashdance . . . What a Feeling
10.	Shout	25.	The Way You Do Things
11.	Man in the Mirror	26.	Put a Little Love in Your Heart
12.	We Are the Champions	27.	Taking It to the Streets
13.	Danger Zone	28.	Takin' Care of Business
14.	The Greatest Love of All	29.	You Ain't Seen Nothing Yet
15.	Footloose	30.	The Heat Is On

Table 3. Most Popular Motivational Songs   *Source:* Clearance Quest (1997).

All sound, then, can be music. *Sonics*, inducing sound with instruments, is an important part of soul-retrieval work and healing in shamanic traditions. Drums, bells, and rattles drove disease from the body, depression from the mind, despair from the soul. The oldest musical instrument to summon the spirit is the rattle, our imitation of rain. The drum is a very ancient instrument; even primates beat resounding objects, much as war drums serve the function of threat display. According to Angeles Arrien in *The Four-Fold Way*, drums can actually produce an altered state of consciousness.

> **MUSIC POINTS**
> - Calibrate "beats per minute" to the effect on heart rate and mood.
> - Draw on other sound effects, such as rattles, drums, bells, or natural sounds, like crashes or sirens.
> - Choose song titles that embellish the theme.

> The drum used in ritual and ceremony "has specific neurophysiological effects and the ability to elicit temporary changes in brain wave activity," thereby facilitating an altered state of consciousness akin to that of yoga and meditation. The psychological experience is one of visual imagery, loss of time, a sense of moving, sudden changes in temperature, feeling energized, relaxed and clear (pp. 166–67).

Music can have mental associations as well as neurophysiological effects. Noise-producing instruments connote certain meanings or are associated with certain experiences, which is different from creating an altered state of consciousness such as that produced by drums. Horns, for example, can be used in place of shouting. Adolph Hitler equipped his Luftwaffe dive bombers with sirens to increase their fearsome effect on the populace. The sound of fireworks, while similar to gunfire, connotes festivity. In most cultures, the bell is associated with spirituality and calling people together, a sonic voice pulling us to our authentic purpose or "calling." Recall the importance of the bell as part of Morehouse College's initiation ritual. The type of music sets the tone for any event and underscores feelings, cultural values, and overall tone.

The Tucson School District in Arizona houses a multitude of ethnic groups. The district works hard to value diversity in order to ensure that its Hispanic,

African-American, Asian, Native American, and Caucasian populations coexist in cultural harmony. Several years ago, all of the district's employees—professional and staff—assembled in one of the city's arenas to kick off the beginning of the school year: several thousand people in one place. The teachers were picketing the event due to a salary dispute, but they were there and their placards carried their message of discontent. One highlight of the event—in addition to balloons, food, and exhibits—was the inclusion of students singing and playing different cultural music—diversity reinforced through song and dance. The event drew the employees together around commonly held values even though they were still divided by the conflict between district budget and individual paychecks.

Movement through Dance

"To dance is to live," said Isadora Duncan, headmistress of her French School of Dance, where young children ate strawberries and expressed themselves in free form in the 1920s.

Dance is a powerful form of nonverbal communication. Dance can be full of spontaneity and emotional expression or planned, as in hiring dancers to organize a country line dance or lead a waltz. People are often more creative on their feet; to move is to lessen anxiety, unless the environment is tense and judgment ridden and criticism is likely. An American Airlines ticket agent tells a story of fears allayed.

> It could have been awkward. We were at an American Airlines function where it looked like they expected us to dance to the band. I have two left feet. A stranger came across the floor and invited me to step out from the sidelines and join in the dance. I resisted, then gave in, only to find myself in the arms of a professional dance instructor. I actually learned a thing or two and didn't look half bad. But who would have noticed—we were all in expert hands that night.

Another possibility is to encourage accomplished celebrants to coach those in attendance who are less accomplished, as happened at the party described on the next page.

I attended a farewell dinner with a group of social workers. They had a DJ, and spontaneously, some of them began a line dance. Others ultimately joined in. It was a memorable evening. The secret was people's willingness to teach and to lead others in the dance.

According to Irenäus Eibl-Eibesfeldt, human dance shows culturally determined differences but also remarkable agreement in form. Exhibition dances display prowess through high jumps, hand clapping, feet stomping, and weapons display. This is true of the Cossacks, the Scottish Highlanders, and the Nilohotohamites. Watch the antics of the winners of major sports events.

Harvey Cox devotes a chapter in his book, *Feast of Fools*, to the widespread use of dance in celebration. He says that dance has its roots not only in pre-Christian and pagan times, but also in early Christianity, where worshippers danced in places of worship, in churchyards, and in cemeteries. As it became taboo in the mainstream faith, dancing went underground and was continued among primitive societies and the poor. It surfaced again in African churches as they admixed their earlier religions with Christianity.

There is a healing quality to movement. Angeles Arrien refers to dancing as the warrior's way of retrieving those parts of the self that are lost or unremembered. Dancing is a method of empowerment and soul retrieval. Dance therapy is a practice that became a formalized treatment in the 1960s and 1970s. The creativity literature tells us that people are more creative and actually make quicker, more high quality decisions on their feet.

Movement and dance are used frequently with autistic kids and other types of emotional "disturbances." Trudi Shoop, a dancer, wrote the book *Won't You Join the Dance?* on the treatment of psychosis, showing the close alliance between motion and emotion. Dancing to her is not a matter of physical prowess and technique, but rather a personally created and styled physical movement that expresses a person's inner being. Preconceived dance combinations, where there is a "right way," can be used as an intellectual defense against the self. Working with psychotics to create their own forms for expression of their feelings, she truly joined them in dance. The objective was to unify mind and body, reality and fantasy, to bring subjective conflict to physical form and make the patient a whole, functioning human being.

> **MOVEMENT POINTS**
>
> - Plan movement at every juncture, even as small as a clap or a wave.
> - Take the chairs away after a meal.
> - Plan a progression that takes the guests from point to point.
> - Leave room for spontaneous movement.
> - Ask people's consent when asking them to join the dance.

Movement can be very sophisticated or as simple as clapping, walking, placing a hand on the heart, shaking hands, or waving. People are more spirited on their feet, and expert party givers know to remove chairs if they want to encourage enlivened interaction. A greeter can serve the function of routing after welcoming; at periodic points people can be routed—from coat check to bar to nibbles to silent auction, point-to-point. Having a mental map helps to create directed and productive energy, freedom within bounds, and a feeling of security. (See Process Flow Map, figure 4, p. 144.)

Putting It All Together: A Poignant Example

To summarize, celebrations must instantly engage our senses, create an opportunity for physical involvement, and then speak to our minds and hearts. Emotional engagement precedes intellectual connection, creating an openness to the deeper symbolic subtext. From food to entertainment, sufficient attention to detail says to the guests, "I am important enough to merit this. I am special." The following example illustrates the construction of a ceremony using all of the features discussed in this chapter.

Cancer Survivors Day

The challenge was to celebrate with gusto those cancer patients who have survived, to commemorate with reverence those who have passed on, and to comfort with tender care the loved ones who have watched a terrible disease take its course. The key feature of the event was the unveiling of five quilt banners made by cancer patients, each square of which told a person's story of battle and triumph over cancer. The common thread—healing hands and hearts—was the brainchild of the Washington Hospital Center's Cancer Institute. These loving mementos are fitting tributes to the Institute's caregivers in appreciation for the love and care extended to patients. (See story on page 105.)

For Nadine Eads, the project leader, the quilt experience and its ceremony represented a sacred calling. In her mind, she saw the ceremony opening with a rabbi, a priest, and a Baptist minister (cancer survivors themselves). Their collective mission: blessing the event and the nobility of the quilt banners. Moving stories told by a survivor, a family member of a survivor, a health-care provider, and a member of the Alexandria Quilters (the collaborating organization) would speak to the meaning of the quilts—the weft and warp of individual and collective, interlacing to form the strength of the communal weave.

The planners sketched the lawn outside the Cancer Center to set the stage—they wanted to see how to seat people to help them feel joined and how to identify survivors. They mapped the flow from greeting to seating, participation, and departure. At some point, they wanted all survivors to stand and recite a statement reflecting the common challenges and triumphs of the cancer experience. Although each person's experience was unique—as represented in the quilt's individual squares—the quilt itself was a shared experience of universal strength and resolve.

What went through the minds of the planners as they designed the event? They let their minds go to imagine the possibilities. Why not release live butterflies? The butterfly is a well-known symbol of cancer's stages of metamorphosis. But a powerful word would need to be said before the release to assure a common interpretation.

Music—they wanted melodic, plaintive sounds. How about Irish? Something beautiful and poignant, sufficiently universal to reach all the participants. They needed an activity to bind the collective. Perhaps all could join in a mutual poem or song: "Amazing Grace" seemed a good possibility. They wanted the overall tone to be that of a joyful celebration of life, embracing also a solemn depth of feeling and reverence.

Thus went the creation of a memorable occasion, as it moved from planning to orchestration. The following thought process summarizes, incorporates, and exemplifies many of this book's themes and principles:

Aim: Celebration of life. Expression of care for others.

Who: Survivors, family, devoted others, caregivers.

Type: Recognition, comings and goings, celebration for others.

Identity: Give survivors center stage. Roles identified with special name tags.

Setting: Nature (on the lawn); nearby chairs in a semicircle; beauty with the quilts.

Design: (1) Invitations and program brochure. (2) Blessing. (3) Storytelling. (4) Informal time at the end. (5) Grand finale with quilt display and butterflies.

Expression: Joy and sorrow, gratitude, remembrance.

Food: Simple refreshments following the ceremony.

Symbols: The quilt, the butterfly, hands, hearts.

Entertainment: Stories told from the heart, open and passionate, made authentic by depth of experience. Spiritual enhancement by religious leaders.

Music: Lyrical, inspirational, neutral. Joining of all in song.

Movement: Ebb and flow of participants. Calling forth of survivors. Release of butterflies. Use of pause and silence and prayer for individual expression of emotion.

Spontaneity: Let the stories be told. Leave space in the agenda for anyone else to speak. Provide informal time at the end for casual social interaction.

Tripwire: The desired butterflies are out of season.

Create the memory trace: Immortalized in quilts with their legends. Take pictures, record the program. Perhaps the media will be invited. Would be good if they were cancer survivors also.

As you can see, the details of forging such an event are part formula, part artistry. But only so much can be planned, and then the muse must take over.

Chapter 12

Improvisation: Releasing Spontaneous Energy

There is little room for compro-
mise around the central issue of planning in the creation of meaningful, memorable celebrations. But in
addition to all of the pre-gala preparation, which has
been our emphasis thus far, there needs to be a powerful element of spontaneity
and creativity. Born of the moment, it is an invitation that comes from the spirit
of the occasion itself. From Judaism, this is the blend of *keva*, the planful, and
kavanah, capturing the moment. The art lies in balancing the deliberate and the
spontaneous, the plan in relation to play. A successful celebration captures both
and results in a spirited occasion that creates collective energy and union—a
shared sense of community.

> **The notes I handle no better
> than many pianists. But the
> pauses between the notes—ah,
> that is where the art resides.**
>
> —Arthur Schnabel

Self-Organizing Celebrations

Human systems, as described by Margaret Wheatley in *Leadership and the New Science*, possess innate properties to reconfigure themselves, to be self-organizing or self-renewing. A self-organizing system has the freedom to grow and evolve into a design of its own. There is only one rule: It must remain consistent with itself and its past—a principle Wheatley calls "self-reference" (p. 135). In celebration, this argues for an initial provocation—a convening, a purpose, a challenge—then standing back, letting go, and allowing participants to design and shape the occasion. What will emerge spontaneously is a new form that makes perfect sense to the participants.

In *Open Space Technology*, Harrison Owen offers us a novel idea for running meetings that originated in his observations of various kinds of gatherings. He noticed that most real stuff at meetings occurred during coffee breaks or over drinks and dinner. So he built a methodology for convening groups that thrives on a spontaneous agenda. A real-life adaptation of Owen's methodology might look something like the Conference for Organizational Transformation (O. T.) celebration, which was described to us by Ward Flynn, an attendee.

> The conference attendees were given the theme for the
> conference celebration—a Western hoedown. At that moment,
> supplies were thrown down—hats, streamers, stars, butcher
> paper, colored paper and markers, lots of tape, sparklers.
> Who will participate in the steering committee, they asked?
> Spontaneously groups began to form—costume, entertainment,
> refreshment committees. There was an element of surprise
> about the celebration. This event is going to happen!
> Something wonderful is going to occur! It was truly creative.
> A wild free-for-all with very little external control. The only
> prearranged piece was a country-western band. We all created
> the rest of it.

A central point here is that true, authentic celebration arises from within a group. It cannot be forced or manufactured. The most expensive, elaborate contrivances, props, or activities will not guarantee a meaningful event. Unless you have the sign-off of the participants and can call up the prevailing spirit of the place, the occasion will turn out empty and barren of joy.

White Space

Every party has its special parentheses, the white space on which celebrants cast their unique imprint and create artful pauses between prewritten notes. Once people arrive, they need a second invitation: to help create the occasion, releasing the subterranean reservoir of collective energy and passion. Martha Stewart describes this well in *Entertaining*:

> A guest impulsively sat down to play a spectacular medley of 1950s ballads—"Wake up, Little Susie" and "Heartbreak Hotel"—and the rest sang along with nostalgic passion. . . . The guests filled up their Baccarat goblets with water to different levels and attempted, like children, to make music. These interesting developments, which eventually made the evenings, were unpredictable, and yet they had something to do with the way a hostess had organized each gathering, with sensitivity to the guest list, with an eye toward a convivial situation. She had, in each case, made everyone comfortable enough to be his own natural, impulsive, expressive, social self (p. 13).

The playfulness, drama, and excitement that emerge spontaneously in rituals and celebrations lie close to the surface in every human group, waiting to be summoned. The requirements include a safe place, enough space to take form, and a little encouragement to get things going.

Learning from Theatrical Improvisation

Improvisation is a tool used by actors and actresses to open up emotional spontaneity. Mac Pirkle, whom we quoted earlier, is director of the Tennessee Repertory Theater in Nashville. The Rep, as it is called, trains stage performers to tap their inner storehouses of emotional expression. We asked Mac to speak with us about the relationship between improvisation and celebration, and following is what he said:

> We have been taught "no" since we were little children. So we rein in our "free spirit," become emotional self-censors. Through a series of structured exercises, such as having actors do stupid things with their voices and bodies, we break rules and have

them observe no consequences from it. . . . I learned "paratheatrics" in a training experience—how to manipulate the minds of people who want to go. I finally learned to appreciate it. This is theater.

In the preparation of actors, the first step is to free them from thinking in terms of right and wrong—to get them to think, "This is just what I do." We create proof of that through some games . . . . We move them differently, do common things in odd ways to disinhibit structure. Next we retrain them not to hide mistakes. For example, in four-part harmony, you have to sing it out to know it's wrong, to fix it.

Regarding improvisation, everything we do (as humans) is spontaneous; we never know what we will say. You have to work with people to manage the excitement when they are really on. . . . It takes something like moving them differently to disinhibit, to tap the emotional storehouse, to access different aspects of the human condition.

In Mac's theatrical world, we see the importance of movement and the use of odd, unfamiliar structures to disinhibit people. Breaking rules is helpful, but it is also important to keep people near to the edge of what is known and comfortable and to foster an environment of trust and supportive values, where fear of failure is discouraged. Creative action is waiting close to the surface, ready to bubble up as it is permitted. But it needs theatrical license and a safe stage in order to come up and out.

In the classroom and with corporate audiences, we have invited participants to develop creative productions—raps, songs, poetry, ads, plays—to dramatize any relevant theme or current issue. Rarely are people given more than twenty minutes to come up with something. The results are truly remarkable—poignant, humorous, and revealing. The art is lying so close to the surface, begging for release. The laughter and poignancy of expression and acceptance binds people in creative enterprise and discovery of each other.

Theater Therapy

Seattle's Virginia Mason Hospital and Clinic has institutionalized theater through the creation of what has been labeled TT—Theater Therapy. The idea was hatched at a retreat several years ago. The administrators' group had not met away from the hospital for a long time, resulting in the buildup of day-to-day tensions and travails that any group of people can produce. After dinner and after a day of meetings and presentations, the nurses put on a farcical theatrical production set to the musical *The Best Little Whorehouse in Texas*. The production had not been planned in advance. It was spontaneously thrown together in the short time between the end of afternoon sessions and the cocktail hour before dinner.

Through songs and skits, all the hospital's latent issues, problems, and conflicts were dramatized and made public. But since theater is the safe space between truth and fiction, the result was a hilarious rendition. It had most of the administrators from the hospital's various functions and departments literally rolling on the floor or doubled up with laughter.

The idea caught on. Now each year at the administrative retreat, the theater is convened after dinner. They create a stage. An emergency room physician (a masterful humorist) puts a diamond earring on his left ear and becomes the official stage director or master of ceremonies. No one knows in advance what will happen. The theatrical bill of fare is created on the spot. People sing songs, act out scenarios, and imitate other managers, physicians, nurses, staff, or executives. In a hilarious two hours, the hospital's issues are aired, appreciated, and often resolved. Through theater, the hospital sees itself. The celebratory atmosphere releases talent and energy, and reinspirits people for another year of dealing with a tumultuous, confused, and rapidly changing health care environment.

Rap Reporting

NRDC, the transformed telephone repair enterprise mentioned earlier, captured an event on video that stirred the spirit of the entire organization. It happened during a companywide business meeting. Each business unit was reporting on its efforts toward turning the troubled company around. Everyone attended—employees, managers, and executives. The spirit of celebration filled the room. One team leader, who expressed a great reluctance to speak prior to the event had them worried. According to Burgess Oliver, CEO of NRDC

> We were afraid that she wouldn't show. She was so nervous about speaking. We thought she would cancel. Then she got up and did this rap. She brought the house down. . . . *She brought the house down*!!

Imagine, as you read her rap below, that she's not the type to get up in front of an audience—especially an audience of employees and executives on a serious occasion. Also imagine that everything she is saying is so very true, known by most everyone but never uttered in public. Imagine her performance as so unlikely that the audience starts clapping along as they realize the truth her rap is expressing.

> We hear the ring
> We take the call
> The customer's important
> So we don't stall.
>
> You need 2500 Silhouettes?
> We don't mind
> If it takes 'til dawn
> We'll get them out on time.
>
> Hey, man
> We can't rendezvous
> We've got work
> That we must do.
>
> We clean 'em and we shine 'em
> And we send 'em down the line
> Beat that schedule
> Every time.

Notice the combination of theater, chant, surprise, and playfulness in this rap with movement (the audience clapped along) that summed up the organization's new climate—a climate artfully constructed by leaders pulling a troubled organization out of insolvency.

When the Party Falls Apart

Nothing is perfect, and so it goes with ceremony and celebration. Despite all the preplanning and fretting about details, something almost always goes wrong, as illustrated in the following story told to us by James Whitehead:

The board of trustees was holding a retirement dinner for one of its members, the president of the University of Virginia. We had built a Japanese tea house and planned a Japanese tea ceremony for the entertainment. And . . . oh, no! Twenty-four hours beforehand, the tea ceremony giver fell ill. We had to fill in the blank. It just so happened it was the Year of the Tiger. Well, there was a zoo twelve miles away. What could they do? Could they supply a caged tiger? Unbeknownst to us, we got a free-roaming Bengal tiger, freshly shampooed and heavily sedated. When guests arrived, the room was darkened, with a spotlight on a Chinese urn in the tea house, flanked by a student in Japanese attire. When all were seated, the lights went out and then up and there sat the tiger in place of the urn, secured by a metal leash hidden behind the door. In walked the trainer, who took the tiger around the room. It thrilled people.

Another story, this time about a wedding:

Every detail of this wedding had been carefully scripted. The reception afterwards was lavish in every detail. There was one problem, however. The caterers had forgotten to chill the champagne, a glitch they noticed just as the guests were arriving. It was a very hot day. I turned to the stressed hostess and told her that the Rothschilds always drank their champagne with a cube of ice. Never have I seen such a rapid uptake of an idea. The party was electric with the specialness of the Rothschilds' unique way to appreciate champagne.

Saturn's remarkable Homecoming event was described in chapter 5, where we mentioned briefly the intense thunderstorm that drenched the event, collapsed tents, created gigantic mudholes, and resulted in several serious injuries. But instead of dampening the festive spirit, the storm accentuated the event's upbeat atmosphere. Two Saturn managers climbed from underneath their collapsed tent and ran toward the parking lot to help people get to their cars or find shelter. As they got to the lot, they realized it was too late. Everyone was totally drenched. Neither umbrellas, raincoats, nor ponchos offered protection against

POINTS ABOUT SPONTANEOUS EVENTS

- Break or bend convention enough to get people out of their molds.

- Give a theme, set some bounds, and then let go.

- Trust participants to help create their own good time.

- Give permission and a push for frolic and fun to emerge.

- Capitalize on what comes up, no matter how seemingly disastrous.

- Move people from their comfort zone onto a safe stage.

the blustery wind and torrential rain. One of the managers took off his poncho, rolled it up, and threw it to his colleague. Minutes thereafter, an impromptu football game was underway. People slogged through the mud, so covered by goo that personal identities were indistinguishable. Those who weren't playing were cheering on the irregular sidelines. Nobody seemed to care about the storm anymore. The game lasted until the storm passed. Everyone was anxious to celebrate the winning team until the realization hit—no one had kept score. A recent Saturn commercial showed shots of the storm—one of the worst in Tennessee's history. The ad ended with the words, "But we were all in it together, the way we always have been."

Tripping the Light Fantastic

Fantasy is "the faculty for envisioning radically alternative life situations." Festivity is "the capacity for genuine revelry and joyous celebration" (Cox 1968, 7). A child shows innate capacity for surprise and joy. These are the vital elements of life that many Western people have lost in the pursuit of a scientific, rational, industrial society built on predictability and control. Cox points to New Year's Eve as an example of our modern festival. To him, it typically lacks verve or feeling. It is often vacuous, frenetic, desperate, anxious, obsessive.

A similar trend is happening around children's birthday parties. What used to be a backyard event, with parents serving homemade cake on rickety picnic tables, has now become a large, expensive production. In an article in the October 1997 issue of TWA's *Ambassador* magazine, Lawrence Tabak comments on this commercialization of birthday gatherings:

> My fear is that [kids] will learn to think of birthdays as just
> another commodity, a purchase as thoughtless as the latest

Barbie or Beanie Baby. When the difference between your
birthday and the next kid's is simply a matter of where you sit at
the same table in the same room with the identical agenda,
you're linking key childhood memories not with family or home,
but with the marketplace (p. 72).

Fantasy entails hope; it is visionary, dreamlike, and made of myth. Unlike a
dream, however, fantasy is constructed by its owner(s) in a creative, conscious act.
As one repair associate at NRDC experienced it:

Imagine this! We arrived at work and there were buses lined up
on the curb. We were told to get on board and away we went to
places unknown. Turned out to be Smiley Hollow, where we had
a picnic in the big barn, danced square dances, and did the
hula-hoop. There was a terrible storm that afternoon but it
didn't matter. No one has ever forgotten that day.

Who is good at fantasy? Children, the mentally ill, and the oppressed. That
includes a lot of people. But most everyone, deep down, yearns for fantasy experiences. Escape through fantasy opens a world of possibilities. Fantasy is essential to meaningful human life. There are far more adults at Disneyland than
children, but chronological age poses no barrier for becoming childlike in Fanta-
syland. As Matthew Fox tells us in *The Reinvention of Work*:

It is through ritual that the young can become excited enough
about their existence to throw themselves into the adventures
of living, learning, relating, forgiving,
letting go, and letting be. Ritual puts
them in touch with generosity of heart,
with the courage and gratitude that will
energize them for the journey (p. 251).

Magic flows through us; mystery infuses
encounters; the fantastic lures the unseen into the
physical world. Invited, we willingly express the hidden and unknown.

POINTS ABOUT FANTASY
• Be deliberate in the use of surprise.
• Surprise yourself.
• Rather than prescribe, allow and encourage the fantastic.

Humor and Merriment

Joel Goodman, author of *Laffirmations—1001 Ways to Add Humor to Your Life and Work*, is a master humorist who recognizes the productive power of laughter in the workplace. Humor is about making life a little lighter and looking at life from a different angle. Sharing humor decreases tension and fuses people in a moment of unself-consciousness. Laughter produces a healthy state of being and is a powerful way to open doors, minds, and hearts.

> **POINTS ABOUT HUMOR**
> - Think funny.
> - Adopt a playful attitude.
> - Be the first to laugh.
> - Laugh with, not at.
> - Laugh at yourself.
> - Take work seriously, but not yourself (p. 213).

Southwest Airlines has built its culture on humor and merriment. Flight attendants have been known to hide in overhead bins and pop out when the passengers arrive. Their in-flight announcements are famous for their irreverence. Agents and attendants have a book of games entitled T.J. LUV *Presents a Guide to Inflight and Gate Games* as a source of outrageous songs, trivia, contests, and games. In their book about Southwest Airlines the Freibergs note that they have observed a childlike quality in the people who work for Southwest—not childish, but reflecting an attitude of playfulness. Their description of the Southwest way to a sense of humor is summarized in the box above.

Creativity: The Core Source

The creativity literature suggests conditions that produce the artistic moment, the profound and practical new insight. Mihaly Csikszentmihaly gave us the idea of *flow* as the optimal human experience. More often experienced in work and in community, flow is a feeling of oneness, effortlessness, joy; it is the creative state of being. It is enhanced by conditions of freedom, absence of fear, minimum surveillance and control, and viable options. Interestingly, in their book *The Creative Spirit*, Daniel Goleman, Paul Kaufman, and Michael Ray say that creativity flourishes in the absence of competition and rewards, which are prized and encouraged by many enterprises. This is not to say that a modest amount of pressure and competition is bad; some people enjoy the challenge of a tight deadline, a huge goal, and worthy competitors. What is destructive to creativity is when these galvanize to create an all-encompassing climate of fear—of being put down, embarrassed, or censured for being "off the wall" or "out of step." Feeling unsupported in trying to be more innovative will short-circuit people's creativity.

As designers of celebrations, we must recognize and challenge barriers to creativity and set an example of openness, imagination, and the capacity for surprise. Creativity is a natural human state; something that allows us to evolve and adapt to changing circumstances.

Creativity on the Spot

During years of teaching both college students and adults, we have observed the rapid production of creative material as part of group exercises when participants are given some ambiguity and the permission to be creative. As already noted, this type of creativity occurs in the production of corporate events when people are given a creative objective—for example, to illustrate a certain learning point—and given a brief amount of time (under an hour, often less than twenty minutes) to put together a message in the form of a poem, song, dance, or theater piece.

One such exercise pertains to designing an awards ceremony to recognize participants in a leadership course. First, students write something they feel proud of on a certificate of self-recognition. These certificates are then scrambled and randomly handed back to participants. Each person is then challenged to invent an awards ceremony for the original certificate holder in only a few minutes. They are to select a prize from miscellaneous paraphernalia—toys, office supplies, and other "stuff"—and then confer the award in a public presentation. The aim of the exercise is to hone the skills of leaders in enhancing pride and spontaneously creating ceremony. But the collateral effect shows itself in the glow of the recipients who haul away their certificates and foolish items with great glee. The actual value of the

---

CELEBRATION SONG
Power and Spirit

Celebrate the spirit within
Transforming the lives that we share

Infectious spirit transcends
Liberating souls to one end

Celebrate all that we are
Celebrate all that we do

Power is the spirit
Spirit is the power
Reach out, it's here

Give it away, let it flow
Let it go, watch it grow

Celebrate loving with power
For there is always tomorrow

Power is a gift that you give
And what you give you receive

Celebrate all that we are
Celebrate all that we do

by Jubal Yennie and Lynn Bercaw
Power and Spirit Class
Fall 1996

prizes is irrelevant; they become symbols of appreciation and accomplishment, proof positive that it costs almost nothing to invent ceremony and festivity on the spot.

Following is an example of a ceremony created on the spot by celebrants. This one is a combination of preplanning and spontaneity at Oasis Center, an agency that serves teenagers. The story was told to us by Sue Fort White, director of development.

> Kwanzaa culminated in a feast on December 13. Everybody contributed a recipe; we compiled the recipes and presented them as a love gift. In the African-American celebration, these love gifts are called *gawadi*, an idea derived from hearts traditionally given by children during the harvest celebration. There were lots of musicians in the agency, many drummers, which created a space of holiness. In the center of the room was a big piece of yellow paper. We invited the memories of those who had an impact on our lives to be present in the hallowed space. We acknowledged with grateful hearts the gifts we had received from our ancestors who had passed before us. Spontaneously, people shared their thoughts and memories and tears; no one was pressured to do so. We talked about the Seven Lessons: unity, self-determination, cooperation, sharing by all, creativity, purpose, and faith. We were to take the best of those principles, celebrate and honor the past, and strengthen our hope for the future. The culmination was a building of community and a sharing of a sense of sacred knowledge. Our gratitude increased for a workplace so human, so authentic, like a family, where we could be ourselves.

Only in a place where there is tremendous trust and respect can people take creative risks in this way, to fill the white space of an open agenda. This event was planned by a multidisciplinary team, with a simple formula, "food–music–memories," orchestrated yet open, with a powerful result.

Celebration is not so much content as it is a permission-giving structure in which to let go. People have to understand the new and different structure in order to improvise. Mac Pirkle has said of actors, "They have to learn their lines in order to improvise emotionally." The creativity comes with the confidence that you know the routine; with more preparation, it is easy to improvise. Celebration planners will want to devise a general structure and always leave room for spontaneity.

> **POINTS ABOUT CREATIVITY**
> - Give party planners and participants permission to be creative.
> - Create an environment absent of fear.
> - Remove the demotivators for creativity: fear, surveillance, judgment, evaluation, pressure.
> - Devise a solid structure and leave room for spontaneity.

Spontaneous Designs

All human beings possess the innate ability and desire to express uniqueness and, at the same time, a lingering wish to be connected: *me* and *we*. Celebratory events offer channels—song, dance, eating, laughing, mourning, telling stories—to express our humanity and aliveness.

The most successful celebrations call forth creative juices, but first, participants need a structure. With the proper support and a gentle push toward fantasy and play, even the most stalwart and steeled executives can become artisans of the festival.

We have called this improvisation. When is improvisation appropriate? Always, if you want the design of *me* in your event.

When we are able to overcome our conditioning and minimize feelings of judgment, embarrassment, and possible humiliation, many spontaneous and beautiful acts emerge from people. These acts will unfold in great, majestic, meaningful celebrations that will not be soon forgotten.

Chapter 13

Creating the Memory Trace

O ften, the most fruitful outcomes of a celebratory gathering come after the event is over. Memories imprint lasting feelings and the legacy lingers as an enduring influence on a culture and its members—a treasured symbolic memory trace that calls up the occasion again and again as needed. A sustaining memory trace is created through stories, videos, and what we call stuff—souvenirs and mementos.

> I remember, I remember
> How my childhood fleeted by—
> The mirth of its December,
> And the warmth of its July.
>
> —Winthrop Mackford Praed

Stories Tell

One of the hallmarks of a cohesive, focused corporate culture is an abundance of stories. Stories help keep alive echoes of celebrations past. Present and future occasions provide opportunities to swap tales—old and new—that will eventually take their place in a company's enduring legacy of legend and lore.

Reflecting back on the stories presented in earlier chapters, it is easy to see how effective celebrations spawn good stories: Saturn's Homecoming and the launch of the company's first automobile; Patsy Bruce's creation for Honda of a life-size replica of the French Quarter in New Orleans in the city's Superdome; the HCA "Big Tent Shuffle"; and the H.M.S. Printafour extravaganza put on by Quad/Graphics. Stories carry the spirit of the event even to those unable to experience the occasion firsthand. Sometimes, as with fish stories, the tale grows larger and larger, surpassing the actual facts in the retelling. Stories are truer than true; their embellishment makes them even better the second or third time around. Good celebrations set the stage for swapping tales that linger as a treasure-house of meaningful exploits and happenings.

The following tale from Longmont United Hospital in Longmont, Colorado, illustrates the point:

> It was a dark and stormy night. We were on a retreat in the Colorado mountains. Some thirty of us health-care leaders were winding down in the lodge, after a day of training. It started with music, dancing, beer, and popcorn. There was a fire blazing in the big stone hearth and a bubbling creek outside. We sat in a group and waited out the silence, until someone offered the suggestion that we share a story. Each person would add on to the story the person on their left had just recounted or elaborated. Then the real tales started coming out. As the physical energy wound down, we began to share some stories and memories of our organization, its people, and its past. To the beat of an African drum we found laying beside the hearth, the stories began to roll out like a flood of memories. As one story ended, another began, embellishing on the first, or completely contradicting it. Pretty soon we were outdoing each

other in dramatized, outlandish tales. Health-care folks, especially nurses, have some wild stories about what happens behind the scenes, particularly when they were young initiates.

For many years, the Beaverton School District in Oregon convened its annual "Pits and Berries" storytelling time at its end-of-summer administrative retreat. At round tables, small groups shared stories about the year's tragedies and travails, "the pits," as well as the high points and successes, "the berries." Each group then picked its top story in both categories and joined another table where the top two of the four stories were chosen. These were then presented in front of the large group. An applause meter would determine the top "pit" or "berry" tale of the year. The following winning story, which gives a glimpse of how storytelling adds to the festivities of the retreat, was told by a school principal:

> I was sitting in my office when a little third-grade boy walked in and gave me a note from his teacher. It said, "Johnny said he would rather suck dog snot than do his homework." I said to myself, "I don't have time for this right now." So I told the little boy, "Wait here, I have to think about this for awhile."
>
> I walked over to the cafeteria to talk with Johnny's grandmother, who is our head cook. I told her about what happened and asked her if she had any ideas about how to handle the situation. While we were discussing options, the school custodian, who was eating his lunch, looked up and said, "My dog's in the boiler room." What a lucky break. I went down to the boiler room and found the dog, a little Lhasa apso with kind of a runny nose. I picked up the dog and went back to my office where the boy was being interviewed by our child development specialist in an attempt to figure out why he would say something like that. I walked over to the boy and put the dog right in front of him—nose to mouth. He looked at me and snorted, "What?" "Go ahead," I said. "What?" he again replied in a sarcastic way. I told him, "Look, you can either go back to class and do your work or suck the snot out of this dog." He smiled slightly and said, "I think I'll go back to class." The

real neat thing is the next day I talked to his grandmother. She told me that at home that night his mother had asked him about his day at school. To which he responded, "I found out today that my principal has a sense of humor."

The story is funny but also very powerful. Its subtext reveals themes of inventiveness and cooperation among administrators and staff, as well as a novel approach to dealing with conflict. It also reveals a lot about life in school. The year-by-year accumulation of such stories is one way the school district reinforces its unique approach to education.

Here is another story with a sad twist told by Bob Pike, who is a trainer.

Talk about beginnings . . . envision a young manager, only thirty-three, promoted up through the ranks to where he was running an entire department of some twenty people, many more senior and experienced than himself. The first day in the new position, wearing his finest, he called his direct reports together for a rallying start. His boss shortly arrived upon the scene, only to interrupt and point out his disapproval of the new leader's clothes—a red jacket and blue-checked slacks. "Why don't you go home right now and put on professional attire," the boss commanded. On the way to the parking lot, the young man decided management was not really his calling. You see, that young man is me.

Many good books have been written to teach storytelling (for example, *Managing by Storying Around: A New Method of Leadership*; *Real People Real Work: Parables on Leadership in the 90s*; *Everyday Heroes*). They suggest keeping stories simple to make a single point as well as borrowing stories and using them to point to values and gently teach. Toastmasters also has advice on the subject of how to deliver a good story.

In their 1988 manual, Toastmasters teaches us that the essence of story-telling is memorization in pictures so that you relay the story in the same pictorial terms. The tools of effective delivery are

★ *Tempo*. Vary the tempo. For example, "Sleeping Beauty" is slow and dignified; "Robin Hood" is firm and strong. Poetic passages or those that require imagination must be delivered slowly.

★ *Rhythm*. Add cadence but not sing-song.

★ *Inflection*. Use the rise and fall of voice to add meaning and emotion.

★ *Pause*. Pause to enhance curiosity and interest, to make transitions, and to allow reflection on meaning.

★ *Volume*. Increase volume to express excitement, surprise, or action. Lower it to add suspense or emotion.

> **POINTS ABOUT STORYTELLING**
> - Be simple, brief, and understandable.
> - Arouse emotion. Tell and act with passion.
> - Teach without lecturing or demanding.
> - Elevate values or morals in the underlying theme.
> - Use friendly, nonthreatening communication.
> - Paint word pictures with descriptive language.
> - Be sincere; tell it from the heart.

The beauty of a story is that it reduces us all to a childlike state—quiet, deeply listening, defenseless, and eager to be swept away by enchanting visions and elevated morals involving deeds well done. The tale spun with emotion and passion transports the audience to another place and time and gently makes its point, as the listener lives out the characters' lives.

Pictures and Videos Portray

Recall the military retirement ceremony described in chapter 7. The event was immortalized in photos—both candid and formal. There was a casual photographer and a formal photographer. Each was assigned different photographic tasks as the occasion unfolded.

In *Managing to Have Fun*, Matt Weinstein suggests capturing glimpses of organizational life through a number of photo safari journeys—setting your people in search of themselves doing novel things or reenacting versions of commercials, like Toyota's "Oh What A Feeling" (pp. 144–147). People love to savor their pasts through pictures. What is the one thing everyone tries to save in a house fire?

Photographs conjure up memories and, like stories, they reveal subtle cultural subtexts. In trying to bring together two very different AT&T divisions in a merger, we used photographs to contrast two unique cultures and meld them into a composite. Unless these different divisions could be knit together, the resulting battles and competition for supremacy would cancel out the obvious strategic and financial advantages of the union.

A transition team composed of an equal number of members from each division was convened. The team's first task was a "field trip" to both offices, accompanied by a photographer. Anyone could request to have something photographed. Later, the pictures were assembled into a collage. The composite showed clearly the unique cultural patterns of each division, one a hard-charging sales group, the other a conservative operations unit. As the transition team reviewed the contrasting composite, someone remarked, "What an odd couple." That became the theme of the subsequent transition ceremony, where film clips of successful odd-couple acts were shown—Abbot and Costello, Martin and Lewis, Burns and Allen. Then the composite was reviewed, set against the elements of culture—values, hero/ines, rituals, and so on. The crowd roared and then got to work discussing how their differences could be put to work in a high-performing "odd-couple" relationship.

Videos provide an even more powerful way to sustain a memory trace of a meaningful cultural event. One striking example of this is the 1991 celebration of the tenth anniversary of Hospital Management Professionals (HMP). The event was held at the Ritz Carlton in Laguna Niguel, California. One hundred hospital

---

POINTS ABOUT PICTURES AND VIDEOS

- Include the informal with the formal.
- Set the group in search of its own pictures.
- Take face shots, with spontaneous expressions.
- Display pictures publicly and give to individuals.

executives and their spouses attended. The three days featured speakers, a black-tie dinner, a visit to Mission San Juan Capistrano, a run on the beach, and an emotional dinner where employees presented the company's two founders, Shelly Krizelman and Bob Huseby, with oil paintings by Niemann.

The company hired a Hollywood film crew to videotape the entire celebration. The night before the farewell event, the film crew worked nonstop in a rented trailer outside the hotel to produce a video that was presented during the final lunch. The video begins with a plane flying over the hotel trailing a banner with the number ten on it. From the plane, footage was taken of the executives at a cocktail party on the hotel grounds. The film proceeds through each activity, with a relevant music score playing in the background—for example, "Chariots of Fire" for the morning on the beach. Each participant received a copy of the video. In 1997, Shelly Krizelman, until recently a senior executive at Quorum (which acquired HMP in 1992), told us, "I still look at the video from time to time. It always refreshes some delightful memories I will cherish forever."

Say It through Stuff

Symbols also create a powerful memory trace. Walk into any manager's office and you will see T-shirts, mugs, picture frames, pens, and other memorabilia, often in company colors. This is the stuff from celebrations of yesteryear. The symbols are a powerful reminder of the event from which the memento came. To see or touch the symbol is to recapture the memory or a significant milestone—and the spirit of an event. The following story is a good example of what we mean:

> **POINTS ABOUT SYMBOLS**
> - Choose images that are tasteful and appropriate.
> - Choose images that reflect a person's role in an event.
> - Find objects that have repeated use or visible aesthetics that beg to be displayed.

I was working with a group of Brazilian executives in a seminar. It wasn't going well, and I couldn't figure out why. So I walked into the men's room with a guy who spoke a little English in addition to Portuguese. He explained the problem. In Brazil, our forefinger-to-thumb a-okay sign is an obscene gesture. Basically, without knowing it, I kept giving them the finger. I went back and let them know that I was not pleased at being kept in the dark for half of a day. I called them Brazilian barracudas. They told me they didn't like American consultants, and particularly they hated the American business cases that consultants bring with them. We cleared the air and got down to business. It was a terrific two-day session. To celebrate the ending and to make sure all was healed, I arranged for a wine tasting and paid for it myself. I taught them how to taste wine and talk about its essence. Then they presented me with a gift—something to remind me that Brazilians are not barracudas. I opened the gift: It was a stuffed piranha. "That's our true essence," they said in unison. I still have that stuffed fish in my office. It keeps a wonderful memory alive.

Create a Record

Paint the Walls

There is a new art form called graphic recording, in which a recorder takes notes in words and pictures as a meeting or planning session is going on. The group can also participate in chronicling the process, expressing their thoughts on the wall charts.

Similar to flip charting, recording in this way creates a "group mind." Then a group memory can be transferred to copies through a keyed transcript. Or some flip charts, overhead projectors, and dry erase boards make these copies mechanically, on the spot.

Storyboarding on walls has been used to create collective histories, such as those used in Future Search Conferences and described by Marvin Weisbord. Storyboarding can also be done in large groups by using small breakout groups to create designs that are collected into an overall group record. Many derivations can be used to honor an occasion.

POINTS ABOUT RECORDS

- Have memory pieces at every celebration.
- Display items for a sense of identity.
- Liven up pictures with stories or stories with pictures.
- Engage participants in creating the record.

Scrapbook the Memories

The scrapbook is a tool for compiling history through pictures, memorabilia, and stories. Some organizations employ a scrapbook method to capture and portray their histories. According to Susan Adamson, Creative Memories consultant,

> The further back you go, the more a scrapbook gives you vision. Who we are has so much to do with where we have come from. Scrapbooks build a sense of identity. People are lacking vision because they lack roots.

Following is the story of how the YWCA in Nashville, Tennessee, prepared to celebrate its one hundredth anniversary:

> We were meeting to plan the one hundredth anniversary of the YWCA, and I was asked to head up the scrapbook committee. There was so much history! How to capture it? We decided to call for contents along with stories to go into a scrapbook early on—to be organized prior to the event. But also to have live, interactive moments at the event itself, to have participants write comments on the pages, capture stories on video and on the wall, and put party pictures of people as they are today alongside the way they were.

An organization's sense of identity or self-reference, as Margaret Wheatley calls it, is enhanced by visual portrayal of symbols. Storyboards, as described above, are one example; museums, wall displays, or photo archives are additional examples. Even documents, letters, thank-you notes, acknowledgments from others, and awards can be scrapbooked.

Symbols Speak

Memories fade without reminders. Complete an occasion with stories, pictures, a video, or scrapbook to create a memory trace—something that plays back the experience again and again. A take-away memento embodies the meaning of a celebration and allows that meaning to be reaccessed whenever a lift is needed. Entire cultures are carried through centuries by symbols, stories, and such stuff. Celebratory corporations will seize this opportunity to build meaning through memories.

Chapter 14
Recipes for Failure

So far in this book we have made suggestions and offered examples for designing meaningful celebrations to fit a variety of situations. Our intent is to motivate people to reinvigorate and reinspire the modern workplace, and there is probably nothing more motivating than an engaging ritual or ceremony. The moment is savored; the memory is cherished forever.

Unfortunately, the flip side is also true. A poorly planned, improperly executed, or ill-timed event produces immediate disappointment or anger and a long-lasting bitter aftertaste. A large budget does not ensure success. Millions of dollars each year are wasted on empty gatherings that leave in their wake a spiritual void and an emotional vacuum. It may seem hard to screw up a festive occasion, but it's done all the time.

In this chapter, we replace our principles for designing successful celebratory occasions with surefire recipes for failure. We wish we could say that we made these recipes up, but in fact, these suggestions for disaster, although presented tongue in cheek, are based on real-life situations we have observed. Our readers could probably add their own "wish-I-could-forget" examples of celebrations that didn't work.

Fatal Flaws

To fail at celebration, try one or several of the following:

★ *Do something because you've always done it that way.*

Don't learn from history.

Don't acquire knowledge from participants about their past experiences.

Go through the motions even though the oomph has long since expired.

★ *Do something new for sheer novelty.*

Find out what everyone else is doing and substitute it for the traditional happening.

Mistake grumblings about the annual event for a unanimous yearning for something new.

Put new, aspiring executives in charge of an occasion without knowledge of what has always been done before.

Hire a consulting firm and give it carte blanche to design the event.

★ *Be unclear about the event's aim.*

Delegate the planning to a low-level assistant or a detached committee composed of people with little else to do.

Get the public relations department, an ad agency, or the marketing department to do it for you.

Mix too many motives: make up for a bad year, pump up your suppliers, thank your customers, impress your relatives (on the company budget).

★ *Misread your audience.*

Use inappropriate symbols, for example, Christmas carols sung to Jewish participants.

> We thought we had a marvelous way to close out our class at the end of December. We set theories and ideas to Christmas music. The students loved it, all except for one student who came up as everyone was gleefully walking out. She said, "You cut me out of the celebration; I'm Jewish."

Neglect traditional details.

Serve alcohol-only drinks in the presence of teetotalers; serve nonalcoholic-only drinks to a mixed crowd, with a majority who are accustomed to a regular cocktail hour.

★ *Forget the buy-in.*

Invent your own version of a good time.

When there are multiple sectors, cultures, nationalities, even locales involved, overemphasize one of them or play to a subset.

★ *Belittle poor performance or make threats.*

The executive's message of fear in the following story may have been understood, but was it appropriate for the annual retreat?

A new executive wanted to create a high sense of urgency among his managers. At the company's annual event, he showed two clips from the movie *Patton* to the one thousand people assembled from around the world. Both clips were repeated nearly twenty times as the frightened, perplexed group tried to sort things out. The first clip showed Patton telling his troops: "Your job is not to die for your country. It's trying to get some other bastard to die for his." The second clip shows Patton relieving an officer of his command in the field and giving it to the first soldier who comes along. "And if you can't engage the enemy, I'll find some other son-of-a-bitch who can."

★   *Treat the event as routine.*

Cut corners. Underfund it. Let the food or drink run out—maybe they'll leave early.

Depersonalize people by disregarding their importance (for example, their name, origin, or role).

In your speech and actions, trump me-me-me or management in general.

Let participants fend for themselves: where to go, what to do.

Even worse, ask the employees to substitute for hired help.

★   *Be inauthentic.*

Say things you don't mean.

Do things that feel hokey and unlike your sense of yourself.

Stick strictly to a script.

Have someone else write your speech.

Give thoughtless gifts.

Create a facade.

A health care executive recently hosted a series of ceremonies designed to accentuate employees' knowledge and appreciation of the hospital's traditions and values. His intentions were noble; the execution left something to be desired. The featured part of the one-day gathering was a speech about the hospital's past, present, and future delivered by the top administrator himself. Employees attended one of the series in groups of two hundred. At the second event, the executive gave a rousing forty-five minute speech. At the end, he asked for questions. None were forthcoming. He pressed the crowd, "You must have questions; don't be afraid to ask." One staff worker rose to his feet. "I have a question: Who are you?" An embarrassed executive put the question to the person sitting next to the first employee, "Tell him who I am!" A red-faced employee shrugged his shoulders, gulped, and said, "I don't know either." By this time, the entire audience was silent. The executive was aghast.

★   *Show false affect.*

In the path of celebration, display an altercation. Take on an opponent while you've got an audience.

> It was an important company event. No sooner than the room was filled, a higher-up created an altercation by picking on a subordinate (kidding but not kidding). The room froze.

Use the event to show you have a tender side, even though you don't.

★   *Destroy the mood with careless comments.*

Use any of a variety of well-known "killer phrases." For example,

> "We've always done it this way."
> "That's too touchy-feely."
> "Let's put it into committee."
> "This is the (company) way."

Utilize energy sappers. For example,

"That won't work."

"What a stupid idea."

"Didn't you get the memo about the dress code?"

At one lavish company gathering, a senior manager strolled up to a new employee who was standing with a group of seasoned veterans. The novice had purchased a new suit for the occasion. It was a lightly checked gray tweed. The manager looked the newcomer over from head to toe and then inquired, "Where did you find a pair of slacks to go with that sport coat?" The youngster then observed that everyone else was attired in a charcoal suit. The others roared in laughter—at his expense. Not much of a festive greeting for a new employee.

★ *Ignore timing.*

Have a celebration before the reason for it, for example, an end-of-semester celebration while people are still stressed over exams.

Hold a ritual of joy too close on the heels of sorrow. In the following case, the timing worked, but only because the planners and participants examined the potential clash and found a sensitive way to go ahead.

It was time for the faculty "get smashed" party, held annually after graduation. But one of our closest colleagues had passed away on the Thursday prior to the party. The mood among us was somber. Should we have it? We decided to think it through from his perspective: What would he have wanted or what would he have done himself? Hold a hell of a party, we all agreed! And that we did, mindful of him—the most engaging and cathartic wake I have ever experienced.

★   *Overplan.*

Give away money or expensive gifts, expecting extravagance to increase the thrill.

Force people to follow a passion that only you have, for example, deep-sea fishing for employees and spouses where most of them get seasick.

> This was the golf game from hell. An executive took his senior staff on retreat to a mountain golf resort in order to build his team. Some did not golf, including the facilitator of the retreat, but went along for the ride in golf carts. Thus began what was intended to be a celebration. A huge thunderstorm swept over the course—severe enough that two trees were ultimately taken down by lightning. The executive, however, was intent on playing even though everyone was drenched, cold, and miserable. And no one would say anything. Finally, the facilitator said, "This is foolish. We need to go in." Later, one of the players thanked her, saying, "We couldn't say something unless you said something. Thank goodness you did." Later, we all drank too much at dinner.

★   *Mandate how (and how not) to have fun.*

Spell out a list of do's and don'ts.

Threaten job loss or major punishment for "doing it wrong."

Come down hard on those who let down their hair a little too much.

Check the advice in this news release from the Associated Press, which was printed in the December 23, 1996, *Tennessean* under the title, "Have Fun, But Don't Be Stupid":

Jack Erdlen, a career consultant, gets phone calls every year after the holidays from companies asking for his help in finding an employee a job. The reason? The worker was fired for his behavior at the office holiday party.

Sometimes workers dress indiscreetly or buttonhole the boss. . . . Others choose to start romances amid the festivities.

To make sure the office party isn't your last, introduce yourself to top bosses but don't criticize others or the company, Erdlen and other consultants advise.

Along with drunkenness and romances, avoid office gossip, inappropriate clothes, and staying too long. And don't monopolize the conversations or raise your voice.

"Have fun, but keep it under control," said Andrew Sherwood, a New York–based human resources consultant. "Let someone else be the life of the party."

★ *Stay aloof.*

Reinforce hierarchy—physically separate the top brass and the lesser privileged.

Leave the greeting to someone else.

Show your official status by arriving late and leaving early.

Be immune from the activities. Let the little people play.

A sales force of a Fortune 500 company arrived for a banquet at a major hotel. There were two entry ways to the ballroom—one for the winners, one for the losers (those who didn't make their quotas). The room was divided by a chicken-wire fence. On the right side, the quota-makers dined on filet mignon, drank Dom Perignon, and listened to a string quartet. Visibly opposite, the losers sat on wooden chairs, drank beer, and ate stale bread.

★   *Ignore past failures.*

When there's obvious attrition from a company event, for example, a picnic, keep the same format.

If the shrimp or turkey is cut from the party and there's an outcry, fail to heed the feedback and fix the mistake.

Do not bother to evaluate events by gathering feedback.

Everything Speaks

No aspect of celebration escapes interpretation. Peel back the party elements and find an attitude, belief, or value the event conveys to those in attendance (table 4).

Celebrants see things the way they want to, which is why entertaining the celebrant as customer or guest is so critical. People look for the symbolic subtext in every celebratory attribute or action. Who among us has not committed at least a few of the aforementioned *faux pas*? If you think of the event participants as guests or customers, your sensitivity to their needs, history, and culture will help ensure favorable calibration of the event's actual message to its intended message. Although we wrote this chapter tongue in cheek, the examples are based on real-life celebrations accidentally scripted for disaster. To avoid costly errors, celebrations need the same level of attention as that given to strategic planning, financial forecasting, and other important business functions.

Action	Separate treatment by rank. Brass arrives late or does not show.
Message	Title/status is what counts around here. The little people do not.
Action	No receiving line or greeters.
Message	Make your own way—sink or swim.
Action	Scale down on the food and/or the setting, especially in a profitable year.
Message	Thanks to your efforts, someone else is going to be wealthier.
Action	Overlook details and personal needs.
Message	You are not valued.
Action	Reading of scripted speeches by leaders.
Message	I had no thoughts on this issue, so someone else had to create my image.
Action	Strict protocol.
Message	Fit in or get out.
Action	Mandatory fun.
Message	I read a book on this or am copying someone else. *-or-* It may hurt, but it's good for us (me), I think.
Action	No celebratory activity at all.
Message	Work is not play—get serious. *-or-* I am fearful of this kind of stuff. I might lose control.

Table 4. Everything Speaks

Chapter 15
The Role of Key Players

Put everyone to work in the [quality] transformation was another of W. Edwards Deming's wise maxims for improving a company's quality performance. His plea for inclusiveness applies just as much to celebration as to the techni-

> **The key to your impact as a leader is your own sincerity. Before you can inspire with emotion, you must be swamped with it yourself. Before you can move their tears, your own must flow. To convince them, you must yourself believe.**
>
> —Winston Churchill

cal aspects of work. There is an important role for everyone in celebration; no one should be relegated to the sidelines.

But someone has to set the stage and orchestrate the process. That is the job of leadership—not leadership that comes from position, but leadership that comes from passion and purpose. That means anyone can step up and lead the parade. Leaders must set the tone and tempo, so all players can play. In short, joy reigns in work only when leaders put their hearts and souls into periodic, meaningful celebrations.

Leaders Are Central

Accordingly, leaders cannot sit on the periphery of celebration. A leader is somewhat like a social director, a cheerleader, a primary keeper of values and culture. James Kouzes and Barry Posner, in The *Leadership Challenge*, see authentic celebration as based on three central principles:

1. A focus on key values

2. Public recognition of individuals and/or teams

3. Leadership involvement

To Kouzes and Posner, one of the key attributes of a leader is the ability to "encourage the heart." To do this, leaders need to take the time to recognize contributions and celebrate accomplishments. The best leaders lead from the heart naturally because they are literally in love with employees, company products and services, and their customers. They schedule celebrations, cheerlead, develop social support networks, and constantly rekindle everyone's passion, purpose, and spirit.

After W. Edwards Deming returned from his journey to Japan, where he taught statistical process control in Japanese factories, he wrote down fourteen principles or maxims for leaders. These are commonly referred to as "The Fourteen Points." His twelfth point concerned the leader's responsibility to remove barriers to joy in work. He echoed this in a similar list of attributes for managers. Managers of people, he felt, should remove obstacles to joy in work by creating interest and challenge, by helping people improve, and by celebrating accomplishments.

Later in his career, Deming distilled his fourteen points to four essential points, which he called Profound Knowledge. Profound Knowledge is a deep (and rare) understanding and appreciation of (1) systems thinking, (2) variation in systems and processes, (3) the application of the scientific method, and (4) psychology. In his last days, he condensed this shorter list to one key idea. He had winnowed his points from fourteen to four to one, each time reaching a deeper level. He told his final point to a close friend: The essence of our work in quality is about the human spirit.

Engaging people's hearts as well as their minds is key to a spirited work-force. Principles for achieving this have become more a part of the leadership literature than ever before: Give people meaningful work; pay them as well as you can; let everyone have a stake in the business; listen so that people can teach you how to lead; engage others in setting the organization's aim (purpose, vision, values); recognize that all are important players and acknowledge them personally; communicate, communicate, communicate; encourage learning and innovation; remove fear and enhance trust; play on the interdependence of all parts of the system by convening teams and groups; embrace diversity, foster differences, and encourage conflict to fuel better ideas; live what you want your company to be (walk the talk). Our addition to this list: Celebrate! We feel celebration is central. Just as the sun is the center of the solar system and its primary source of energy, so too is celebration the primary source of energy in an organization.

If this is true, why don't leaders rush to celebrate? We outlined some of the reasons in the first chapter, but let's examine in greater depth the excuses leaders have for not paying more attention to celebration at work.

Two Primary Excuses: Ignorance and Fear

We think there are two primary reasons why leaders hesitate to celebrate: (1) leaders do not know how to celebrate, and (2) leaders are afraid to celebrate. This book is an attempt to deal with the first, and we are hopeful that leaders will enlist the help of others where their knowledge leaves them short. The second reason is a curious one: What is there to fear? We had a conversation with Kathleen Ryan, who with Daniel Oestrich wrote *Driving Fear Out of the Workplace*. She contributed some practical wisdom on the matter.

> The key issue is control. As a nation, we are very conflict
> avoidant. We fear losing control. Control seems necessary to
> people when they don't trust each other. Many business
> organizations have social occasions where there are precise
> guidelines. The need for protocol stems from the lack of belief
> that I can trust others and myself to behave in the right way.

In bureaucratic, top-down organizations, fear is a major instrument of control. Kathleen Ryan went on to say

> You talk about surprise, delight, joy, creativity—new territory for
> a company celebration. How can you do that when you're
> watching your backside?

In *Intellectual Capital*, Thomas Stewart says that the work environment of the Industrial Age has been supplanted by the work environment of today's Knowledge Economy. He lauds General Electric's Work-Out program—a never-ending series of town meetings at which employees propose changes in work processes and bosses must approve or reject them on the spot—as a model of the new way.

> Programs like Work-Out succeed because they provide safe
> places where people can share ideas about work without being
> shut down by bosses and bureaucrats. To use more of what
> people know, companies need to create opportunities for
> private knowledge to be made public and tacit knowledge to be
> made explicit (p. 88).

The antidote to fear is open communication, which has its place in celebration.

Other Excuses

There are a host of excuses used by leaders for not celebrating, but we think most of these probably mask the two excuses we have identified as primary: ignorance and fear. Cover messages may sound like what we describe below.

We Don't Have Time

Chances are good that many leaders will shudder at the prospect of additional time required to add fun and festival to an already overly ambitious list of responsibilities. Burgess Oliver, CEO of NRDC, a telephone repair division of Nortel, calculated that it takes six weeks to make up the backlog from shutting down the plant for one day for the division's hijinks. Saturn Corporation closes for one day a month, knowing it means that a number of cars won't be produced. Both noticed, however, that employees voluntarily began to adjust their work to salvage time for celebration. They worked harder to make up for lost production time so that they did not fall behind on short-term productivity.

We Can't Lose Face

Many leaders are reluctant to celebrate due to the risk of failing or losing face. It's one thing to blow a meeting or screw up a strategic decision. It's quite another to sponsor a celebration that falls flat or flops. Staying inside the lines breeds a sense of security that, while often an illusion, provides a certain comfort. Workers, likewise, will be unwilling to revel or reveal their playful, passionate side if they sense they will have a price to pay later on. Sure we can let our hair down and have some fun, but is someone watching and taking names? Better to stay in place and keep to the tried and true. Be a robot at work and a human at home. It's difficult to imagine celebration in the face of this kind of fear.

Leaders have to be willing to let go and trust the process. A good setting of the stage, enough forethought to orchestration, and sufficient pause to permit spontaneous participation almost ensure a celebration that will create itself. Given the right encouragement, even the stiffest financial managers or engineers can become the wildest, most exuberant party goers.

If everything doesn't go as desired, leaders can ask, "What happened? How can we do this better?" It's a matter of staying close to employees, listening, and learning.

This Is a Business, Not a Playground

By now it should be apparent that we believe fervently in two age-old maxims: "People who play together stay together," and "Play pays." If you still disagree, call employees of some of the companies cited herein and see how they feel about the role of celebration in the workplace.

It's Not for Us

Some leaders may truly believe that celebration does not fit into their culture, but those same leaders are the major shapers of that culture. As James Collins and Jerry Porras put it:

> The essence of a visionary company comes in its translation of its core ideology and its own unique drive for progress . . . into *everything* that the company does (p. 201).

Celebrations tailored to the organization's identity weave abstract values into activity so that people can experience, appreciate, and applaud what the company stands for.

It Costs Too Much

Celebration does not always have to be high cost. Low-cost and no-cost solutions are sprinkled throughout this text. (See chapter 8 for ideas.) Sometimes spontaneous, grow-your-own celebrations have more meaning than a host of overly orchestrated meetings designed by upper management. (See chapter 12 for ideas on improvisation.)

Enablers of Celebration

The wise leader will play on his or her own strengths and enlist the talents of others in planning and orchestrating ceremonial events. Very often, it's not the formal leaders who have a knack for knowing how to put together an engaging, meaningful occasion. Every company has an unofficial group of party planners who, given some resources, encouragement, and a lot of leeway, can come up with something spectacular.

The Informal Network

Very often the best enablers of celebration are well-known players in the informal cultural network. Priests or priestesses are the primary keepers of company history and the faithful watchdogs of company values. They are indispensable when it comes to planning ritual and ceremony. Their knack of knowing just the right tone and feeling helps create an event that reflects a company's historical roots, acknowledges present realities, and projects a meaningful future vision. Gossips provide the "real stuff" about what went on at last year's celebrations. They are also excellent sources of information about what's currently on people's minds. Storytellers light up when an event is underway. They should be encouraged and rewarded handsomely for sharing legend and lore during the festivities.

People-Oriented People

Some people are more given by their nature to acts of celebration. These are the outgoing personalities, the other-oriented folk, who can become part of a family that works hard and plays hard. Herb Kelleher, CEO and "High Priest of Ha Ha" at

Southwest Airlines, believes in starting off on the right foot—*hiring* people with the proper spirit. These bundles of energy with big hearts then vie for the vaunted and valued places on Southwest's Culture Committee. Jana Lewis, marketing director for Southwest's Nashville station, summed it up:

> At Southwest, we look for attitudes: people with a sense of humor who don't take themselves too seriously. Our training provides specific skills, but the one thing Southwest cannot change in people is the attitudes people bring with them.

In hiring party bartenders and waitresses, Martha Stewart, who offers some gems among her rules, believes in employing young actors and writers whose interests are in meeting people, in activity, in potential "material." The enablers need to be "people" people.

The Celebration Specialist

There are celebration specialists and special events planners who are professionals experienced at making events work. Consultation with such a planner is likely to ensure success when the inside cast of characters needs a boost. Planning a celebration is not a job to foist on people who don't have a passion for creating something special.

Figure 5 shows a single page of a specialist's plan, called a critical path. Outside masterminding of this sort can free the organization to do what it does best—imprint the occasion with its unique cultural stamp.

A Cadre of Celebrators (Call It a Committee?)

Releasing the design of celebration to insiders is a true act of empowerment. It gives participants a chance to stretch their imaginations and draw from their hearts. It provides them with an opportunity to create gifts for others. If they are seen as having gifts to give, they will produce wonders. A true test of leadership is the leader's ability to find the gifts that people have to give, invite people to give those gifts, and then honor the result when they do.

Some examples of celebration planned by committee include Southwest Airline's Culture Committee, which was created for the sole purpose of perpetuating the Southwest spirit. The committee draws together more than one hundred shamans, spiritual teachers, storytellers, and other cultural players from across

WHAT	WHO	WHEN
Charter team to create anniversary event	Sr. Mgrs.	week 1
Meet with team to discuss concept and clarify roles and timeline	Sr. Mgrs. and Team	week 2
Review similar past events and interview employee customers	Individual and Employee Reps	week 2
Theme choice and dress code	Team	week 3
List invitees: (Include families? significant others?)	Team	week 3
Locale search: Parking? Valet? Atmosphere? Distance? Other team criteria	Team and Subcommittee	week 3–5
Secure date	Appointee	week 5
Invitation design	Corp. Comms.	week 6
Plan and secure entertainment: Proposals, Auditions	Subcommittee	week 6–8
Caterer—search and hire	Subcommittee	week 6–8
Photographer—search and hire	Subcommittee	week 6–8
Sign final contracts	Team Leader	week 8
Aesthetics: Flowers, Music, Decor, Mood	Team	week 9
Map flow of guests: Process flow map, Seating chart, Parking/valet	Team	week 10
Select and coach presenters	Team, Sr. Mgrs., and Speakers	week 11
Memento planning and procurement	Team	week 12
Press coverage	Team Leader	week bef. event

Figure 5. Celebration Event Worksheet

the company's diverse functions. These are the company ambassadors, working behind the scenes to keep the company's spirit alive. The committee meets four times a year, all day, to plan ways to perpetuate their unique vision, values, and philosophy.

Southwest's Culture Committee is similar to the Disney department called Cast Activities, which is dedicated solely to providing picnics, games, and other events for employees. Its main mission is to create a sense of team spirit, camaraderie, and fun. At NRDC, a telephone repair company mentioned earlier, the TOPS Committee is made up of employees authorized to give "spot awards" of $100, a luncheon ticket, or a T-shirt when they spot something that deserves special recognition.

Two final examples of committees are the Ritual Committee of the Institute for Transpersonal Psychology in Palo Alto, California, and Ben and Jerry's Joy Gang. The Institute's Ritual Committee consisted of a rotating group of students who selected seasonal occasions (such as Halloween, Solstices, Thanksgiving) and built community spirit through creative celebrations. Out of the blue, they would also place flowers, cards, candy, and the like on people's desks.

Ben and Jerry's Joy Gang, a permanent committee with a similar mission, keeps life at Ben and Jerry's hopping and full of fun. A full-time coordinator and ten to twenty volunteers work to create perpetual spontaneity—grants to buy joy-enhancing stuff, like candy and flowers—and to sponsor special events and contests capturing the energy of everyone in the six-hundred-person organization. The key message: "Be creative and be yourself!"

Celebration: Everyone's Job

Celebration thrives on the active involvement of many people. It never happens, however, without the commitment and enthusiasm of an organization's leaders. In celebration, the vision, values, guiding principles, norms, and heroes of a culture are displayed to be heeded and appreciated by everyone—irrespective of official rank or salary level. It is important to remember that the subtleties in a celebration carry the message of who and what counts.

Leaders can take courage in pursuing celebration by paying attention to the ideas and tools needed to help create uplifting occasions. But leaders must remember that while leadership can provide support, encouragement, and resources, it is most often others who make great events happen. A leader's job is to give permission, to encourage a safe space. Followers are then free to express their joyful, creative selves. Celebration is an act of art and of the heart and will not be miscalculated if it comes from deep within individuals and from the shared values a company holds most dear.

Chapter 16
Recapturing Joy at Work

Our nation's workforce has grown weary with lean and mean, management-for-profit tactics. A growing hunger for meaning and purpose amidst chaotic change has spawned a wealth of literature on soul, spirit, and simplicity. Bring back the

> There is nothing better for a man than he should eat and drink and that he should make his soul enjoy good in his labor. This I have seen in the hand of God.
>
> —Ecclesiastes 2:24

people-side of business, they seem to say. But where does the energy for the

people-side of business come from? We believe it comes from celebration. Cele-

bration is at the center, not the periphery of business. It is the sacred fuel needed

to draw out the spiritual resources that enhance performance. It is not idealistic

fluff. It is the real stuff of both achievement and fulfillment. It is encouraged by many successful organizations and found in nearly all great work. Celebration is a natural, human expression of joy and attachment.

Celebration comes in a multitude of forms of ritual and ceremony. There are a variety of reasons to celebrate, and each festive act must be shaped in the mold of a company's unique style and culture. Sometimes we toast triumph; other times we gather in grief. But whether sizzling or solemn, our moments in celebration are at the heart of being human and doing business. It has been said that work is about doing; the soul is about being.

Many companies have already recognized that people need play and purpose in order to produce profits. The evidence is in; we presented it in chapter 1. Examples of spirit-filled companies abound and are peppered throughout this text. These companies and their leaders have had the courage to step out in search of better ways to tap human potential. They have given people an opportunity to show what they can do when committed, motivated, and excited about work.

For example, a Kansas hospital team gathered together recently. In a get-to-know-each-other warm-up, the facilitator asked the members to describe their most memorable moments at work. Following are some of the replies:

> Saying good-bye to my old staff (I may cry). The party they gave me.

> The first day at the new hospital. It was a birth—a new department, a new team.

> My first delivery of a baby.

> My first day on the job.

> The announcement when the CEO resigned. This occurred again recently.

> My grand exit from a job—right into a mop closet.

Most of these memories are of beginnings and endings, gains and losses. These events leave their imprints on minds, whether poignant, sad, miraculous, or foolish. There is a vulnerability in these transitions that begs to be filled with meaning—celebration and ceremony fulfill that need.

In her study of linguistics, Loretta Malandro noticed the following morphology: the first four letters of the word culture are *cult*. Both words are derived from the Latin term *colere*, which means "to nourish or to grow." The word cultivate comes from the same root as culture and agriculture. And what does a culture grow? People. A culture gives form to spirit, meaning to people, and vitality to life. The true meaning of cult is "devoted attachment to principles and beliefs." In business culture terms, this devoted attachment creates corporate commitment and loyalty to a common purpose. It can also be referred to as team spirit, the momentum in any human endeavor.

The ultimate business of business, as W. Edwards Deming stated in his final days, is the human spirit—giving people a chance to grow, flourish, and produce modern miracles. Spirit is not objectively measurable, but it can always be felt, particularly in its absence. Directed and focused communal energy produces results and success. Depressed, tense, fear-ridden environments are self-limiting and rarely nurture the growth, creativity, or capabilities of people. Spirit cannot be legislated or mandated, but it can be cultivated through cultural forms. And particular among these is the age-old act of celebration: ritual and ceremony that nourish play, purpose, and profit at work. When we stop singing, dancing, and storytelling, we begin to lose touch with our hearts and souls. We lose touch with each other. We forget why we're putting in time at work. We concentrate on padding our portfolios, hoarding our power for the sake of getting ahead, or scoring points with higher-ups at the expense of our peers.

Our primary purpose in writing this book is to call attention to this neglected aspect of business. Celebrations are one of the best ways we know to grow spirit and communicate meaning, faith, and hope to those who want more from work than a paycheck. This is not an off-the-wall pipe dream. It's just solid business sense.

Effective celebrations are well-crafted processes that embrace and honor the participants. They are fashioned around a theme, employing all the cultural elements of ceremony and festivity—music, aesthetics, space management, authentic communication. They are full of emotion. They weave people together, allowing freedom within structure. Celebrations have a soul of their own; they summon spirit and so mark the minds of all with a lasting memory.

Successful celebrations speak to all aspects of a human being; they touch people on every level.

★ *Sensorially (Sight, Sound, Taste, Smell, Touch)*
Who is present
Music and sound effects
Silence
Lighting
Aesthetics and decoration
Food
Dress

★ *Physically*
Greeting and routing
Transportation
Joining in singing, chanting, clapping
Dancing
Walking

★ *Intellectually*
Name tags and introductions
Entertainment
Learning
Speeches

★ *Emotionally*
Symbols, talismans, gifts
Recognition and acknowledgment
Tempo of events
Theater
Humor
Storytelling
Memories
Values
Networking

★   *Spiritually*
Uniting the parts as one whole
Addressing higher-order needs
Inspirational speeches
Silence and prayer
Common purpose
Affirming the importance of the individual in the whole

Ten Guiding Principles for Moving Celebrations

We have distilled ten principles for those who wish to invoke ritual and ceremony at work.

1. *Reasons Abound*. There is always a reason to celebrate and no limit to the ways to do it. The effects of ritual and ceremony on commitment, energy, and loyalty, as well as the bottom line, are well documented.

2. *Corporate Connections*. Like whole cloth, celebration weaves together past and future, joins friend to friend, anchors person to place, links leaders and followers, fuses heart to soul, and unites body and spirit. All become part of a cohesive enterprise, creating something of value for others.

3. *Celebration Woos Celebrants*. There is no prescription, formula, or checklist for making an exalting event. The success of a celebration is derived from intimate knowledge of the corporate culture and individual celebrants—what for them constitutes fun, provokes feeling, fosters freedom of expression and permission to be, infatuates, promotes affiliation, and taps their spirits.

4. *Apart and a Part*. Celebration includes and holds each person apart as important and special, while also honoring and reinforcing the community they are a part of. It satisfies our individual longing to be unique as well as our yearning to become one with others in a common culture.

5. *Transports Participants*. Good celebration uses every cultural vehicle to connect, affirm, and fulfill the collective enterprise with meaning, hope, and purpose. It captures the physical, mental, and emotional aspects of being, but touches especially the heart. It takes people from their mundane daily world to a spirit-filled space of shared sentiments and dreams.

6. A *Forum for Creativity*. Celebration invites the fire of the creative spirit that lies so close to the surface, awaiting permission and a free space for expression.

7. *Balancing* Keva *and* Kavannah. Celebration is an art that is both planned and spontaneous; it plays on the calculating (*keva*) and spontaneous (*kavanah*) expression of life. Good celebrations have a script but provide parentheses for improvisation.

8. *Everything Speaks*. No attribute or action of a celebration escapes interpretation. Each action, symbol, speech, or detail signals an attitude, belief, or value. The subtext of a well-planned and executed ceremony speaks to the soul and implants deep messages that linger long after the event is over.

9. *Play Pays*. Successful companies celebrate well—and those who play together, stay together, and work together. Dividends are profitability plus an enlivened workforce. High levels of morale, commitment, and a sense of purpose and camaraderie prevail when celebrations are frequent, focused, and authentic.

10. *True Celebration Must Arise from Within*. Celebration cannot be forced or manufactured. Each act of celebration is unique, and the signature of the celebrants is "the design of me in that." Leadership offers celebration a chance for the collective spirit to be summoned and appreciated.

Releasing Human Potential

Writing this book has given us renewed confidence in people and in the organizations where they work. Too often, we tap only a small fraction of what individuals and groups can accomplish. Unlimited potential is shut off by rigid policies, petty politics, widespread pessimism, and meaningless work. But we have experienced the full majesty of human potential in the spirit of celebration that lurks beneath the surface in both individuals and workplaces.

The problem is that too often in America's companies not enough of people is going into products and services. One of the reasons for this is that sterile workplaces never tap, therefore never profit from, people's full potential. The secret to success is creating cultural forces that allow people to put their hearts and souls into what they do. And one of the most effective ways of doing this is to create celebrations that unite people in a common enterprise and bind them to the value of their work. Harvey Cox put it very well in *Feast of Fools*:

> We have pressed [modern people] so hard toward useful work
> and rational calculation that [they] have all but forgotten the
> joy of ecstatic celebration, antic play, and free imagination.
> [Their] shrunken psyches [are] just as much the victims of
> industrialization as were the bent bodies of those impoverished
> children who were once confined to English factories from dawn
> to dusk (p. 12).

We can no longer afford this waste of human potential. The costs are too high. We have a responsibility to act as stewards of our precious human resources. We need to celebrate and reinvigorate the workplace with play, purpose, and joy. That's the most promising avenue for a vibrant, profitable workplace.

To write this book, we had to see the world through new eyes. Everywhere we looked there was celebration—more and more stories to tell. The latest we heard, before the ink dried, was the tale of an Easter parade down a hospital corridor, with a hat contest. Employees scrambled to create and show off head adornments made of bed pans, flower pots, trash cans, gloves and germs, and stuffed rabbits and monkeys.

What is the message? Is it that employees should be allowed to wear anything they want on their heads? No, the message is that only in a culture of trust, where people experience openness and joy in their work, can there be such play. Play begets work begets play until they are one and the same. People connected in such vitality are, for the moment, one. They are connected in the much larger realm of creativity, aligned with purpose and meaning. They are free to be. Profit is a natural consequence. There is nothing more rewarding than joy in work.

The challenge before us is to elevate our deep inner resources of feeling, connectedness, and higher purpose through celebration at work. In the words of Gangaji, a pupil of Sri Ramana Maharshi, whom we heard speak in Nashville, Tennessee, in October 1997:

> Celebrate that which cannot be taken away—the truth of what is—the force, the grace, the power that is within you.

REFERENCES

Armstrong, David. 1992. *Managing by Storying Around; A New Method of Leadership*. New York: Doubleday.

Arrien, Angeles. 1993. *The Four-Fold Way: Walking the Paths of the Warrior, Teacher, Healer and Visionary*. San Franscisco: Harper.

Autry, James. 1995. *Life and Work: A Manager's Search for Meaning*. New York: Avon-Books.

Baylor, Byrd. 1986. *I'm in Charge of Celebrations*. New York: Aladdin.

Block, Peter. 1993. *Stewardship: Choosing Service Over Self-Interest*. San Francisco: Berrett-Koehler.

Bolman, Lee G., and Terrence E. Deal. 1991. "Leadership and Management Effectiveness: A Multi-frame, Multi-sector Analysis." *Human Resource Management* 30 (4): 509–34.

Bolman, Lee G., and Terrence E. Deal. 1995. *Leading with Soul: An Uncommon Journey of Spirit*, San Francisco: Jossey-Bass.

Bolman, Lee G., and Terrence E. Deal. 1997. *Reframing Organizations: Artistry, Choice, and Leadership*. San Francisco: Jossey-Bass.

Breathnach, Sarah Ban. 1995. *Simple Abundance: A Daybook of Comfort and Joy*. New York: Time Warner.

Canfield, Jack, Mark Victor Hansen, et al. 1996. *Chicken Soup for the Soul at Work*. Deerfield Beach, Fla.: Health Communications, Inc.

Carey, Diana, Judy Large, Cornelie Morris, and Sylvia Mehta. 1982. *Festivals, Family and Food*. Gloucestershire, England: Hawthorn Press.

Castoro, Amy. 1995. "A Passion for Service Excellence." *Credit Union Management* 18 (6): 28–30.

Chappell, Tom. 1993. *The Soul of a Business*. New York: Bantam Books.

Cheaney, Lee, and Maury Cotter. 1991. *Real People Real Work: Parables on Leadership in the 90s*. Knoxville, Tenn.: SPC Press.

Collins, James C., and Jerry I. Porras. 1994. *Built to Last: Successful Habits of Visionary Companies*. New York: Harper Business.

Colwin, Laurie. 1988. *Home Cooking: A Writer in the Kitchen.* New York: Alfred A. Knopf.

Conari Press, eds. 1993. *Random Acts of Kindness.* Berkeley, Calif.: Conari Press.

Covey, Stephen R. 1991. *Principle-Centered Leadership.* New York: Fireside.

Cox, Harvey. 1969. *Feast of Fools: A Theological Essay on Festivity and Fantasy.* Cambridge: Harvard University Press.

Csikszentmihaly, Mihaly. 1990. *Flow: The Psychology of Optimal Experience.* New York: Harper and Row.

Deal, Terrence E., and Allan A. Kennedy. 1982. *Corporate Cultures: The Rites and Rituals of Corporate Life.* Reading, Mass.: Addison-Wesley.

Deal, Terrence E., and William A. Jenkins. 1994. *Managing the Hidden Organization: Strategies for Empowering Your Behind-the-Scenes Employees.* New York: Warner Books, Inc.

DeBono, Edward. 1973. *Lateral Thinking: Creativity Step by Step.* New York: Harper and Row.

Deming, W. Edwards. 1986. *Out of the Crisis.* Cambridge, Mass.: MIT Press.

Deming, W. Edwards. 1993. *The New Economics for Industry, Government, Education.* Cambridge, Mass.: MIT Press.

Depree, Max. 1989. *Leadership Is an Art.* New York: Bantum Books.

DePree, Max. 1992. *Leadership Jazz.* New York: Doubleday.

Douglas, Mary. 1972. "Deciphering a Meal." *Daedulus* (winter): 61–81.

Eibl-Eibesfeldt, Irenäus. 1970. *Ethology: The Biology of Behavior.* New York: Holt, Rinehart and Winston.

Fisher, Julie, ed. 1994. *Southern Living's Holidays and Celebrations.* Brimingham, Ala.: Oxmoor House.

Fox, Matthew. 1994. *The Reinvention of Work.* San Francisco: Harper-Collins.

Frangos, Stephen J. 1996. *Team Zebra.* New York: Wiley.

Freiberg, Kevin, and Jackie Freiberg. 1996. *NUTS: Southwest Airlines' Crazy Recipe for Business and Personal Success.* Austin, Tex.: Bard Press.

Fulghum, Robert. 1995. *From Beginning to End: The Rituals of Our Lives.* New York: Ivy Books.

Gerstner, John. 1994. "Good Communication, Bad Morale." *IABS Communication World* 11 (3): 18–21.

Gibran, Kahlil. 1966. *The Prophet.* New York: Alfred A. Knopf.

Glanz, Barbara A. 1996. *Care Packages: Dozens of Little Things You Can Do to Regenerate Spirit at Work.* New York: McGraw-Hill.

Gluckman, Perry, and Diana Reynolds Roome. 1990. *Everyday Heroes.* Knoxville, Tenn.: SPC Press.

Goldblatt, Joe Jeff. 1990. *Special Events: The Art and Science of Celebration.* New York: Van Nostrand Reinhold.

Goleman, Daniel, Paul Kaufman, and Michael Ray. 1992. *The Creative Spirit.* New York: Dutton.

Goodman, Joel. 1995. *Laffirmations—1001 Ways to Add Humor to Your Life and Work.* Deerfield Beach, Fla.: Health Communications, Inc.

Hampden-Turner, Charles. 1990. *Creating Corporate Culture: From Discord to Harmony.* Reading, Mass.: Addison-Wesley.

Hemsath, Dave, and Leslie Yerkes. 1996. *301 Ways to Have Fun at Work.* San Francisco: Berrett-Koehler Publishers.

Huizinga, Johan. 1971. *Homo Ludens: A Study of the Play Element in Culture.* Prague: Mlada Frontd.

Kidder, Tracy. 1981. *The Soul of a New Machine.* Boston: Little Brown.

Kinni, Theodore. 1996. *America's Best: Industry Week's Guide to World-Class Manufacturing Plants.* New York: Wiley.

Kohn, Alfie. 1993a. *Punished by Rewards: The Trouble with Gold Stars, Incentive Plans, A's, Praise and Other Bribes.* New York: Houghton-Mifflin.

Kohn, Alfie. 1993b. "Why Incentive Plans Cannot Work." *Harvard Business Review* (September-October): 54–60.

Kotter, John P., and James L. Haskett. 1992. *Corporate Culture and Performance.* New York: Free Press.

Kouzes, James M., and Barry Z. Posner. 1990. *The Leadership Challenge: How to Get Extraordinary Things Done in Organizations.* San Franscisco: Jossey-Bass.

Kouzes, James M., and Barry Z. Posner. 1993. *The Credibility Factor: How Leaders Lose It, Why People Demand It.* San Francisco: Jossey-Bass.

Labbich, Kenneth. 1996. "Gambling's Kings on a Roll and Raising Their Bets." *Fortune,* 22 July, 80–85.

LeBoeuf, Michael. 1985. *The Greatest Management Principle in the World.* New York: Putnam.

Loeb, Marshall. 1995. "Ten Commandments for Managing Creative People." *Fortune,* 16 January, 135–36.

Malandro, Loretta. 1995. *The Power in Empowerment: Creating the Future You Want.* Scottsdale, Ariz.: Malandro Communications, Inc.

Maslow, Abraham. 1968. *Toward a Psychology of Being.* New York: D. Van Nostrand.

Metrix Factors. 1988 (December). Tryon, N.C.: Metrix.

Mintzberg, Henry. 1994. *The Rise and Fall of Strategic Planning.* New York: The Free Press.

Moore, Sally B., and Barbara G. Meyerhoff. 1977. *Secular Ritual: Forms and Meaning.* Amsterdam: Van Gorcum.

Neave, Henry R. 1990. *The Deming Dimension.* Knoxville, Tenn.: SPC Press.

Nelson, Bob. 1994a. "Let the Good Times Roll." *Incentive* 168 (6): 51–53.

Nelson, Bob. 1994b. *1001 Ways to Reward Employees.* New York: Putnam.

Oakley, Ed, and Doug Krug. 1993. *Enlightened Leadership: Getting to the Heart of Change.* New York: Simon and Schuster.

O'Neil, John R. 1993. *The Paradox of Success: When Winning at Work Means Losing at Life.* New York: G. P. Putnam.

O'Toole, Jack. 1996. *Forming the Future: Lessons from the Saturn Corporation.* Cambridge, Mass.: Blackwell Publishers.

Owen, Harrison. 1997. *Open Space Technology.* San Francisco: Berrett-Koehler.

Passero, Kathy. 1996. "Songs That Lift Your Spirits." *First for Women,* 16 September. Englewood Cliffs, N.J.: Bauer Publishing Co. L.P.

Peters, Tom, and Robert Waterman. 1982. *In Search of Excellence.* New York: Harper and Row.

Pfeffer, Jeffrey. 1994. *Competitive Advantage through People: Unleashing the Power of the Work Force.* Boston: Harvard Business School Press.

Rechtschaffen, Stephan. 1996. "Twenty-Five Ways to Make More Time for Yourself." *New Woman* (April): 96–101.

Reynolds, Renny. 1992. *The Art of the Party: Design Ideas for Successful Entertaining.* New York: Viking Studio Books.

Rice, R. Eugene, and Ann E. Austin. 1988. "High Faculty Morale." *Change* (March/April): 50–58.

Roddick, Anita. 1991. *Body and Soul.* New York: Crown Trade.

Roddick, Anita. 1994a. *Anita Roddick Speaks Out on "Corporate Responsibility."* West Sussex, England: The Body Shop.

Roddick, Anita. 1994b. *Anita Roddick Speaks Out on "Spirituality and Service."* West Sussex, England: The Body Shop.

Ryan, Kathleen. D., and Daniel K. Oestrich. 1991. *Driving Fear Out of the Workplace: How to Overcome the Invisible Barriers to Quality, Productivity, and Innovation.* San Franscisco: Jossey-Bass.

Sabbagh, Karl. 1996. *Twenty-First Century Jet: Making and Marketing the Boeing 777.* New York: Simon-and-Schuster-Trade.

Sanders, Betsy. 1995. *Fabled Sevice: Ordinary Acts, Extraordinary Outcomes.* San Diego: Pfieffer & Co.

Schein, Edgar. 1985. *Organizational Culture and Leadership.* San Francisco: Jossey-Bass.

Senge, Peter. 1990. *The Fifth Discipline: The Art and Practice of the Learning Organization.* New York: Doubleday and Company, Inc.

Shaper, Donna. 1989. *A Book of Common Power: Narratives against the Current.* San Diego: Lura Media.

Sheehy, Gail. 1974. *Passages: Predictable Crises of Adult Life.* New York: E. P. Dutton & Co.

Sherkenbach, William W. 1991. *Deming's Road to Continual Improvement.* Knoxville, Tenn.: SPC Press.

Shields, Jody. 1996. "Invitation to the Ball." *Vanity Fair* (November).

Shoop, Trudi. 1974. *Won't You Join the Dance? A Dancer's Essay into the Treatment of Psychosis.* Palo Alto, Calif.: National Press Books.

Spector, Robert, and Patrick D. McCarthy. 1995. *The Nordstrom Way: The Inside Story of America's #1 Customer Service Company.* New York: Wiley.

Stewart, Martha. 1982. *Entertaining.* New York: Clarkson N. Potter.

Stewart, Thomas A. 1997. *Intellectual Capital: The New Wealth of Organizations.* New York: Doubleday.

Stoddard, Alexandra. 1989. *Living Beautifully Together.* New York: Doubleday.

Terkel, Studs. 1972. *Working.* Chicago: Avon Printing.

Tice, Lou. 1993. "Lessons in Leadership." Presentation at the University of Alabama Continuing Lecture Series, Birmingham, Alabama, 24 June.

Toastmasters International. 1979. *Advanced Communication and Leadership Program: Specialty Speeches*. Santa Ana, Calif.: Toastmasters International, Inc.

Toastmasters International. 1984. *Communication and Leadership Program*. Santa Ana, Calif.: Toastmasters International, Inc.

Toastmasters International. 1988. *Advanced Communication and Leadership Program: Storytelling*. Santa Ana, Calif.: Toastmasters International, Inc.

Trice, Harrison M., and Janice M. Beyer. 1993. *The Cultures of Work Organizations*. Paramus, N. J.: Prentice-Hall.

Tunstall, W. Brooke. 1985. *Disconnecting Parties: Managing the Bell System Breakup, An Inside View*. New York: McGraw Hill.

Vance, Sandra S., and Roy V. Scott. 1994. *Wal-Mart*. New York: Twayne Publishers.

Weatherford, J. Melver. 1985. *Tribes on the Hill: The U.S. Congress Rituals and Realities*. New York: Bergin & Garvey Publishers.

Weinstein, Matt. 1996. *Managing to Have Fun*. New York: Simon & Schuster.

Weisbord, Marvin. 1987. *Productive Wokplaces: Organizing and Managing for Dignity, Meaning, and Community*. San Franscisco: Jossey-Bass.

Weisbord, Marvin, and Sandra Janoff. 1995. *Future Search: An Action Guide to Finding Common Ground in Organizations and Communities*. San Fransciso: Berrett-Koehler.

Wheatley, Margaret. 1992. *Leadership and the New Science*. San Francisco: Berrett-Koehler.

Whyte, David. 1994. *The Heart Aroused: Poetry and Preservation of the Soul in Corporate America*. New York: Doubleday.

Williamson, Marianne. 1992. *A Return to Love: Reflections on the Principles of a Course in Miracles*. New York: Harper Collins.

ABOUT THE AUTHORS

TERRENCE DEAL has spent a lifetime trying to connect knowledge and wisdom with the everyday realities of the workplace. His many careers—laborer, truck driver, police officer, school teacher, principal, district office administrator, professor, business consultant, and speaker—have grounded his ideas solidly in real-world experience. Job variety has put him in close touch with people from all walks of life. His consulting practice has touched many Fortune 500 companies as well as school districts, universities, hospitals, military organizations, religious orders, and a variety of other types of organizations in America, Mexico, Canada, South America, Europe, the Middle East, Japan, and Southeast Asia. Examples include the Swiss Army, Columbia HCA, several religious orders of the Catholic Church, the Baptist Sunday School Board, New York City Public Schools, Aetna, Pepsico, the Illinois Department of Transportation, Honeywell, Liechtenstein Global Trust, American Federation of Teachers, Naval Weapons Center, Sandoz, Nissan of America, Aerojet, The National Institutes of Health, American Bar Association, H. B. Fuller Company, AT&T, NYNEX, Digital Equipment, Eastman Kodak, Rockwell International, IBM, Intel, Berwind Industries, Anheuser-Busch, and Willis Corroon.

His academic career has included appointments at Stanford and Harvard. He is currently a professor of education and human development at Vanderbilt University's Peabody College. He holds a Ph.D. from Stanford University in education and sociology.

Deal's seventeen books include: *Corporate Cultures* (with Allan Kennedy), *Reframing Organizations* (with Lee Bolman), *Leading with Soul* (with Lee Bolman), *Managing the Hidden Organization* (with Bill Jenkins), and *The Leadership Paradox* (with Kent Peterson). Many of his books are available in multiple languages and have become best-sellers. In addition, he has written over one hundred articles. Both his career and his writings reflect his deep reverence for the power that symbols and culture exert over the human experience. He sees ritual and ceremony playing a central role in organizations of the future.

M. K. KEY is, at heart, a designer and an artist. She paints, plays music, fashions interiors, and composes wardrobes. She received her Ph.D. in psychology from Vanderbilt University. Her twenty-five year career in health care has cast her in many positions: chief of program evaluation at the Tennessee Department of Mental Health and Retardation; director of program evaluation at Dede Wallace Mental Health Center; senior manager at Dede Wallace; founder of Shibui Corporate Communication and Graphic Design; director of human resources and corporate communications for Commonwealth Oil and Gas; director of research and development for Equicor; and vice president of the Center for Continuous Improvement at Quorum Health Resource Inc. She is now president of Key Associates, LLC.

Her experience has led to her love: quality. For the past eight years, she has traveled widely consulting and teaching. Her courses include Creating Customer-Mindedness; The New Look of Leadership: The Inside-Out Approach; Creative Tools and Methods for Innovation; The Art of Facilitating Teams; Conflict and the Art of Intervention; Architecting Culture: Creating an Environment for Success; Leading Process Improvement Teams; and Planning from the Future: An Integrative Approach. Her teaching extends into the academic community at Vanderbilt University, where she holds an adjunct appointment.

She has written over thirty articles on leadership, facilitation, continuous improvement, change management and conflict, and mediation. She has coauthored two books: *Thought Packages That Produce Results: Just in Time Models for Continuous Improvement* and *The Manual for Designing Change in Health Care.*

Along with Deal, she has observed firsthand the powerful, creative forces that are released when people are supported and invited to participate—whether it is in the classroom or in the corporate world. Her work with executives and managers demonstrates how meaningful ritual and ceremony can be created on the spot.

INDEX